TRAVEL BY PULLMAN

JOE WELSH & BILL HOWES

MOTORBOOKS

First published in 2007 by Motorbooks, an imprint of MBI Publishing Company, Galtier Plaza, Suite 200, 380 Jackson Street, St. Paul, MN 55101-4810 USA

Book design and editing by Mike Schafer, Andover Junction Publications, Mendota, Illinois. Layout by Kevin J. Holland, type&DESIGN, Burlington, Ontario. Technical production and assistance by Wendy Yegoiants and Tanya Anderson, Andover Junction Publications, 2004.

ISBN-13: 978-0-7603-3200-9
ISBN-10: 0-7603-3200-2

Printed in Hong Kong

On the front cover: A rare view of the *George M. Pullman* shows the car sitting at the Chicago Great Western facilities in Oelwein, Iowa, on June 12, 1950. Two years later, CGW purchased the car. Note that it now rides on six-wheel trucks and sports a Pullman "pool" livery of solid gray accented by white stripes. *Harry Stegmaier Collection*

On the frontispiece: Baltimore & Ohio's *Emerald Waters* reflects well the evolution of the steel heavyweight sleeping car. Built as the 16-section *Euclid in 1918*, it was remodeled in 1931 with 10 regular sections and 4 experimental private (enclosed) sections. In 1939, the car was rebuilt with 8 sections and 4 double bedrooms and upgraded to "Betterment Car" status with exterior streamlining (including skirting and full-width diaphragms), contemporary interior features, tightlock couplers, and an upgraded braking system. Renamed *Emerald Waters*, the car entered B&O in 1948, leased back to Pullman, further modernized, and used in various B&O and pool services until it was sold to the C.P. Huntington Chapter of the National Railway Historical Society in 1966. The car has been preserved and is currently on display at the B&O Railroad Museum in Baltimore. In this 1965 photograph, *Emerald Waters* is being switched by the Louisville & Nashville after arriving in Louisville on a Kentucky Derby Special. *Harry Stegmaier*

On the title page: Late in 1961, the Pullman sleeper-buffet lounge-observation car of the eastbound *North Coast Limited* is at speed southbound on the Chicago, Burlington & Quincy main line along the Mississippi River bluffs near Savanna, Illinois. *Phil Weibler*

On the back cover: The *National Limited* was originally a Jersey City-Washington-St. Louis train, but was cut back to Baltimore in 1958. As patronage dwindled, the *National*'s consist correspondingly shrunk, although the *River* cars remained until June 1965, except for periods between 1962 and 1964 when they were replaced by other sleeper-lounger cars. *Alan Bradley*

Contents

Acknowledgments

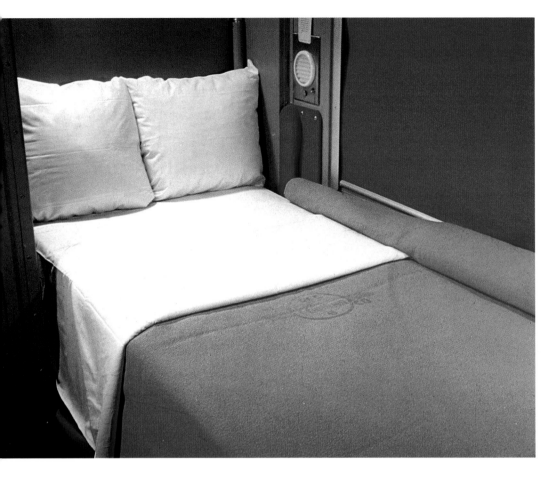

Your own room, your own cozy bed, and your own window with a view of the passing world. Few forms of transport were as comfortable and such as a Pullman car. *THE PULLMAN COMPANY, WILLIAM F. HOWES JR. COLLECTION*

A book project is like a symphony. The author may be the conductor taking the final bow, but much of the credit goes to the folks with the instruments. In this case, the accomplished "musicians" were contributors near and far. Some are old friends and some we've never met.

Art Peterson was instrumental in providing many wonderful heavyweight Pullman builder's photos as well as classic black-and-white images from the lens of Alfred W. Johnson. Friend Jim Beckwith provided numerous rare name-train advertisements. Bill Kratville and Keely Rennie-Tucker of the Union Pacific Railroad Museum unearthed choice images from the Union Pacific archives. Harry Stegmaier Jr. and Alan Bradley contributed rare color car photos from their impressive collections. Pullman expert Robert Wayner provided sage advice, including the name for this book. The Smithsonian's William Withuhn guided the authors through the process of acquiring rare photos from America's premier museum. Arthur Dubin lent key illustrations from his magnificent collection. Kevin Keefe, of Kalmbach Publishing Company and a former editor of *Passenger Train Journal*, wrote the Foreword. Noted artist Mitch Markovitz created beautiful original art which summarized the feel of Pullman like no one else could.

Other individuals who helped include: John Dziobko, Ellen Halteman, Bruce Heard, Kevin Holland, Richard Humiston, Jim Hutzler, Dave Ingles, John Kuehl, John Krug, Bob Liljestrand, Al Lind, Mac McCarter, Jackie Pryor, Trina Purcell, David Salter, Bob Schmidt, George Speir, Jay Williams, Doug Wornom, and Karl Zimmermann.

Companies and organizations that provided assistance include: ACF Industries; the California State Railroad Museum; Cal's Classics; the Denver Public Library, Western History Collection; the Krambles-Peterson Archive; Milwaukee Road Historical Association; the Newberry Library; the Smithsonian Institution; the Railway & Locomotive Historical Society; and the Union Pacific Railroad Museum.

Special thanks for efforts above and beyond the call of duty go to the behind-the-scenes "crew" who promoted, designed, and created this book. To producer Andover Junction Publication's Steve Esposito for hiring us, for his leadership, his sense of humor and for his cash and to his partner Tanya Anderson for her patience, organizational and retouching skills, and good humor; to AJP's Mike Schafer who is quite possibly the best railroad book designer on the planet, and to Kevin Holland, a scholar and a gentleman who does superb layout. And to AJP's Wendy Yegoiants for having the immense patience it takes to work with authors and book designers.

Last but not least, our families and friends deserve special mention: To Janis, Katie, Kellie and Kevin we extend our gratitude for your patience and love.

Joe Welsh, Auburn, Washington
Bill Howes, Jacksonville, Florida
June 2004

Foreword

Imagine a company that fabricated huge steel vehicles as adeptly as it folded crisp linens and towels for thousands of overnight guests. A company that attempted to build a uniquely patriarchal community for its employees, only to call on federal troops when utopian dreams ran afoul of real wages. A company that, for better or worse, became a monopoly and placed itself on the fault lines of America's racial history. And a company whose marketing genius made its name synonymous with an entire product classification long before Xerox came to mean "photocopiers" and Kleenex came to mean "facial tissues."

The company, of course, is Pullman. For more than a century, The Pullman Company was the American traveler's overnight host. On any given night in the decades before the 1960s, thousands of railroad sleeping-car passengers were treated to Pullman's legendary on-board service, usually in cars built in Pullman's own plants. Beginning in 1867 with the visionary ambitions of its mercurial founder, George M. Pullman, and ending with the production of the last Pullman-Standard passenger car in the 1980s, Pullman and its descendant companies wrote a unique and unassailable chapter in American business history.

And yet it has taken so many years for this story to be told the way it should be told. My company has a fine railroad library, and a recent check of the card catalog turned up 37 books about Pullman. But almost all of them concerned some niche or subchapter of the Pullman story. Most are aimed at railfans, with technical information about cars and car assignments. A couple of them tackle Pullman's singular involvement with African-American workers. There's at least one biography of George M. Pullman. But none attempts to wrap the entire enterprise into a comprehensive, comprehensible whole.

Until now. With *Travel by Pullman: A Century of Service*, Bill Howes and Joe Welsh have done the Pullman Company proud. Their richly detailed and visually stunning effort constitutes a significant new contribution to the literature of the American passenger train.

Pullman's story hardly could be in better hands. In Bill Howes, we have one of passenger railroading's great professionals. A former director of passenger services for Baltimore & Ohio, longtime executive with CSX Transportation and a one-time member of the Pullman Company's board, Howes is uniquely qualified to put Pullman in perspective. His collaborator, Joe Welsh, has in recent years assembled an impressive list of magazine bylines in *Trains*, *Classic Trains*, and *Passenger Train Journal*, and book credits that include *By Streamliner, New York to Florida* and *Pennsy Streamliners: The Blue Ribbon Fleet*.

Together these writer/historians have provided us with a book that is long overdue. It's all here, from George M. Pullman's first *Pioneer* sleeping car of 1865 to his poignant death in 1897, not long after a bloody standoff between his workers and federal troops on the streets of Pullman, the town. You'll learn how Pullman pioneered in the hiring of African-Americans and how A. Philip Randolph formed the Brotherhood of Sleeping Car Porters, the nation's first important black labor union. You'll find out how, at its peak in the 1920s, Pullman served 100,000 guests every night, or as many as 36 million in a single year. And you'll learn how Pullman designed and constructed a staggering variety of rolling stock, from the classic heavyweight dreadnoughts of the early twentieth century to the flashy post-World War II lightweight cars that (temporarily) held the public fascination.

Although the full experience of traveling by Pullman is gone forever, it's possible today to enjoy a fleeting taste of it. Amtrak offers a semblance of the experience in its Superliner and Viewliner sleeping cars. Some overnight cruise trains and charter private cars emulate Pullman, although by their exclusive nature they fly in the face of Pullman's mission to provide accommodations to a mass market.

Sad to say, there will never be another company like Pullman. The world is too impatient for its version of civilized overnight travel. But thanks to Messrs. Howes and Welsh, we have a vivid testimonial to the era when the traveler chose Pullman and, late at night, followed the company's admonition: "Quiet is requested for the benefit of those who have retired."

Kevin P. Keefe
Trains *Magazine*
Milwaukee, Wisconsin
May 2004

Introduction

One of the longest-lived companies in American history, The Pullman Company, served the North American travel market from 1867 to 1968. Incorporated in Illinois in February 1867 as Pullman's Palace Car Company, the organization was renamed The Pullman Company in 1900.

Although it was an integral part of American passenger railroading for over a century, Pullman was not a railroad. It owned no tracks aside from those at its own shops. It possessed no powerful steam locomotives or road diesels. And although it owned complete trains, it never operated them itself. Rather, The Pullman Company owned or leased a large fleet of sleeping and parlor cars that was made available to the railroads under contract. The railroads handled the reservations and carried you from place to place aboard your Pullman car.

Pullman was essentially a giant hotel company. In its heyday by the end of the 1920s it operated 9,800 cars staffed by 10,500 porters, attendants, and maids. During the high point of travel in the 1920s, Pullman carried as many as 39 million passengers per year, nearly one-third the population of the United States.

Pullman's job was to maintain, staff, and distribute its cars wherever needed by the railroads. The company's wide-ranging services once extended to Mexico, Canada, and every nook and cranny of

the continental United States. At one time, for example, it was possible to board a Pullman in West Yellowstone, Montana, and end up in Florida without changing cars or trains (although the car itself was transferred between different trains of different railroads). Even tiny lineside communities received their own Pullman service via an innovation known as the "set-out" sleeper. Patrons could board or alight their Pullman car set out at their local station. Asleep in their berth, the only suggestion that their journey had begun or ended was a gentle tug as their car was added to or removed from a train en route from its point of origin to its final destination city.

What made Pullman a success in terms of operation was its organization and attention to details. This was a company that could smoothly keep thousands of guests,

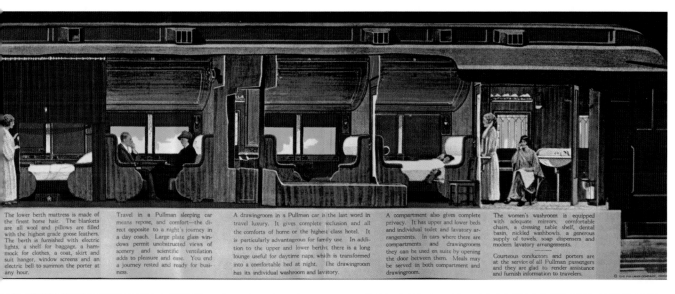

The lower berth mattress is made of the finest horse hair. The blankets are all wool and pillows are filled with the highest grade goose feathers. The berth is furnished with electric lights, a shelf for baggage, a hammock for clothes, a coat, skirt and suit hanger, window screens and an electric bell to summon the porter at any hour.

Travel in a Pullman sleeping car means repose, and comfort—the direct opposite to a night's journey in a day coach. Large plate glass windows permit unobstructed views of scenery and scientific ventilation adds to pleasure and ease. You end a journey rested and ready for business.

A drawingroom in a Pullman car is the last word in travel luxury. It gives complete seclusion and all the comforts of home or the highest class hotel. It is particularly advantageous for family use. In addition to the upper and lower berths there is a long lounge useful for daytime naps, which is transformed into a comfortable bed at night. The drawingroom has its individual washroom and lavatory.

A compartment also gives complete privacy. It has upper and lower beds and individual toilet and lavatory arrangements. In cars where there are compartments and drawingrooms they can be used en suite by opening the door between them. Meals may be served in both compartment and drawingroom.

The women's washroom is equipped with adequate mirrors, comfortable chairs, a dressing table shelf, dental basin, nickled washbowls, a generous supply of towels, soap dispensers and modern lavatory arrangements.

Courteous conductors and porters are at the service of all Pullman passengers and they are glad to render assistance and furnish information to travelers.

BELOW: Justifiably proud of the massive behind-the-scenes efforts it made to provide sleeping- and parlor-car service, Pullman produced this pamphlet in the series to explain the phenomenal amount of laundry needed to support a fleet of thousands of Pullman cars. THE PULLMAN COMPANY, JOE WELSH COLLECTION

railroad cars, and employees in constant motion long before the age of computers. Pullman excelled at minutiae because it had to. To ensure that you had crisp sheets to climb between, for example, Pullman—self proclaimed as "the world's greatest housekeeper"—laundered 284 million pieces of wash per year in the 1920s at an annual cost of over $3 million.

Pullman's on board service was also second to none. Its conductors, porters, maids, and attendants were trained to a fault on how to greet passengers, how to correctly pour a drink, how to properly waken a sleeping passenger, and so forth. It was this remarkable quality and uniformity of service, then largely provided by African-Americans and Filipinos, that was the company's greatest asset to its passengers.

Continued on page 16

PULLMAN FACTS No. 3

THE WORLD'S GREATEST HOUSEKEEPER

ABOVE: Two pamphlets in the "Pullman Facts" series produced by Pullman explained how it built and lighted its cars. The company spared no expense in the use of splendid graphics to tell these stories. *THE PULLMAN COMPANY, JOE WELSH COLLECTION*

RIGHT: Until 1929, when it was bumped by the *Empire Builder*, Great Northern's top train from Chicago to the Pacific Northwest was the *Oriental Limited*, operated by the GN and CB&Q. Striding nobly through the middle of La Crosse, Wisconsin, on Burlington's passenger main through the city on a summer day in 1928, the *Limited* embodies the glories of 1920s railroading, including steam for motive power and a long rake of heavyweight Pullmans punctuated by a high-windowed observation car. *A. W. JOHNSON, KRAMBLES-PETERSON ARCHIVE*

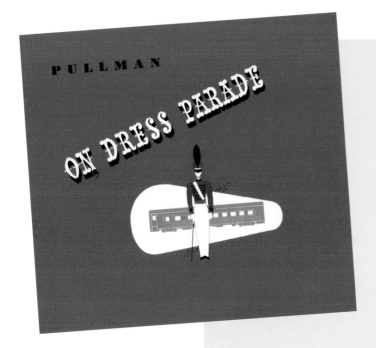

PULLMAN

ON DRESS PARADE

Although we have emphasized the things you'll find *inside* your Pullman car, there is even more to be seen from your Pullman *window*. Here are the rugged hills and fertile valleys, mountains and plains, villages and farms of America—brought close and intimate through the magic of Pullman travel. Inside and out, there is a constant parade of pleasant contributions to your comfort and peace of mind when you ●

RIGHT AND BELOW: Pullman produced an elaborate booklet called *Pullman on Dress Parade* in 1948. Virtually every accommodation offered was explained in day and in night configuration through clever use of a day/night artwork background. They are presented on these and the following two pages for the reader to refer to whenever types of accommodations are mentioned elsewhere in the book.
KEVIN J. HOLLAND COLLECTION

BELOW: Section accommodations were the signature of Pullman travel prior to World War II. BELOW RIGHT: The space-saving duplex roomette in which an overlapping room design helped squeeze more rooms into a typical car. They were located on both sides of a car served by an aisle down the center.

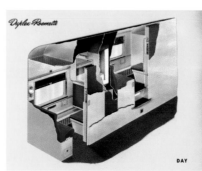

. GO PULLMAN

BELOW LEFT AND BELOW: Two types of roomettes (Pullman's most popular and most common postwar accommodation for single occupancy) are shown in these pair of day/night illustrations. The type A roomette had the fold-down sink on the wall opposite the sofa seat; the type B roomette had a sink that folded down from the aisle wall and over the toilet.

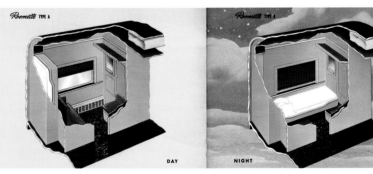

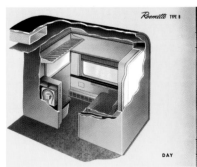

Continued from page 11

To the railroads, Pullman provided economy of scale. To meet heavy seasonal demands, Pullman's national pool of sleeping cars could be reallocated to handle demand for travel to Florida in winter and to the American West in the summer. Pullman also excelled at supplying equipment to handle special moves and unexpected events. In addition to providing cars for special train service, Pullman could, on short notice, create hundreds of extra "hotel" rooms on the ground in "Pullman Cities" when the likes of a convention exceeded a community's ability to handle the demand for hotel space.

Reliability was another Pullman asset. Pullman maintenance was known to the railroads to be second to none.

This orderly world in which Pullman was a primary provider of transportation began to collapse with the advent of the Great Depression in late 1929. Suddenly the great company, which had once enjoyed a virtual monopoly in its market, began to lose money as people stopped traveling or shifted to less costly means such as travel by railway day coach or chair cars, buses, or private auto.

World War II intervened in this steady decline. As it had in World War I, Pullman played the role of unsung hero. It was estimated that 125 million passengers—including troops—traveled 98 billion miles in Pullman cars during the conflict. At war's end, over 5.5 million veterans would reach home in a Pullman between November 1945 and June 1946.

But at that time, a different kind of war was just beginning. The inroads of government-supported auto and airliner transport coupled to inflation proved a deadly combination for the labor-intensive railroad passenger industry after World War II. In 1956, Congress created what became the Interstate Highway System,—a move that would change the way millions of Americans traveled. The airliner, which had risen in popularity significantly since World War II, got a huge boost with the debut of domestic jet service in 1958. Pullman was an early harbinger of the railroad passenger problem. The company's ridership dropped by over four million between 1949 and 1956. More importantly, with one exception (1948), Pullman's average annual operating expenses exceeded its operating revenues every year from 1946 to 1968.

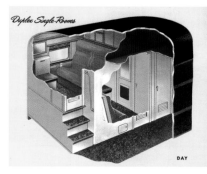

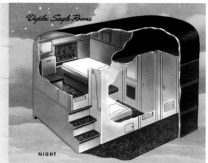

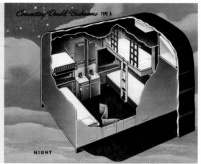

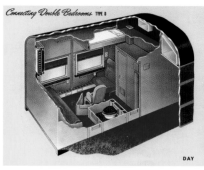

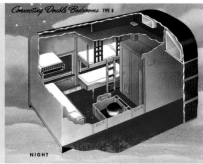

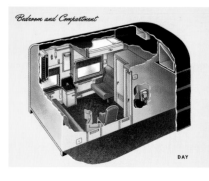

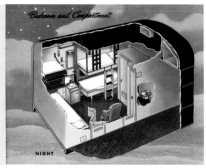

RIGHT: A duplex single room for one traveler overlapped adjacent rooms as in a duplex-roomette car but was wider and featured a crosswise (to the direction of travel) bed. Because of the extra width, duplex single rooms were located along only one side of a car, with the public aisle along the other.

RIGHT: Connecting double bedrooms in various configurations were a virtual suite on wheels for a family traveling by Pullman. Two adjoining rooms could be made into one by folding back the partitions that separated the rooms. A type A double bedroom, found on early streamlined cars, had a toilet that folded into a cabinet under the sink.

RIGHT: Type B connecting double bedrooms were a great improvement over type A and C bedrooms in that they offered an enclosed toilet annex. Individual movable chairs rather than sofa seating were provided for day use.

RIGHT: A compartment and a double bedroom made up en suite was about the most spacious and luxurious accommodation for three or four people. By day you had a combination of sofa-type and individual seats; by night, there were four beds, two transverse to the rails and two parallel to the rails (the case for either will forever be argued by travelers).

Like Pullman, the private railroad passenger industry appeared headed for extinction. As embattled railroads continued to terminate trains and services, Pullman with its massive overhead costs in shops, fleet, and personnel fell further into trouble. But despite the challenge, the great company refused to compromise its standards. Into the late 1960s, on those trains where Pullmans still ran, it was possible to enjoy a quality of first-class service that far exceeded that available at the local hotel next to the interstate or on board a 707.

Nevertheless, the speed of the airplane and the convenience of the interstate eventually defeated the private railroad passenger train. For example, in the jet era the average flight from Philadelphia to Chicago took a little over two hours. Despite wonderful first-class service, the same trip by rail in a Pullman took about 14 hours. For Pullman's primary customer, the businessman, there was no question which way he'd travel in an era where time was money. In 1945, Pullman operated over 5,500 cars; by 1968, when it closed its doors to passengers, it ran just 425 cars. By mid-1969 Pullman would go out of business in the United States and Canada after 102 years of service.

So why write a book about a company that couldn't keep up with the times? Because Pullman provided the finest travel experience that was ever available to the average American. The history of The Pullman Company marks the best effort of a great American company to offer a transportation service where "First Class" meant so much more than just an extra inch of seat width on the five-hour flight to somewhere. And the company did this for a century.

A symbol of an earlier, more relaxed time, Pullman also epitomized the level of quality that can be achieved when a determined group of people put their hearts and minds into a job. The legacy of Pullman's service remains a fond memory for those who have ridden its cars. To those who never had the chance, we invite you to climb aboard in these pages and imagine yourself snuggling down under crisp linens in your berth and watching the snow-covered landscape drift by in the moonlight.

—*Joe Welsh and Bill Howes*

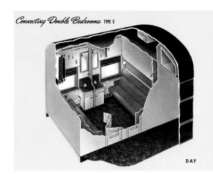

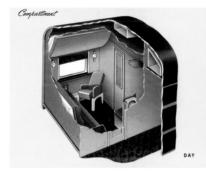

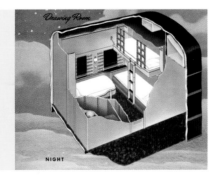

LEFT: A bedroom and compartment suite was a favorite of three- and four-person parties traveling together. Sleeping four but with the ability to have one room made up for day seating and another with the beds made down, they were ideal for parents traveling with children. Of course, the space charge included the cost of both a compartment and a bedroom.

LEFT: Although the term "compartment" is sometimes used—incorrectly—interchangeably with that of a bedroom, a true Pullman compartment slept two in a space larger than a double bedroom. As illustrated here, early compartments in lightweight cars did not have a private toilet annex.

RIGHT: Virtually identical to the type A connecting double bedroom, the type C bedrooms offered enhanced passenger amenities such as additional storage space, full-length mirrors, and slightly longer beds.

LEFT: The drawing room slept three in a spacious room that included a private toilet annex. Aside from the rare, shower-equipped master room (not illustrated) featured on a few premier trains, the drawing room was the largest single Pullman sleeping accommodation offered.

The story of George M. Pullman and his railway sleeping-car system is more about one man's grand vision, marketing prowess, financial maneuvering, obsessive control, and self promotion than it is of technical skill and invention. There had been sleeping cars on the railways for some 20 years before Pullman entered the business, but he saw a need to redefine the service and went about single-mindedly to implement his vision, drawing liberally on the work of others along the way. His enterprise became one of the largest and most successful in the nation's history, lasting for more than 100 years, before its demise in the wake of new technologies and changing travel preferences. For a period, "Travel by Pullman" was a part of the American way of life, and it left an indelible mark on America's social history and culture.

It is generally accepted that the wooden rectangular body of America's first sleeping car was 34 feet long and 8 feet wide, had seating for day travel and three-tiered bunk-style berths for night, was named *Chambersburg*, and ran on the Cumberland Valley Railroad between Harrisburg and Chambersburg, Pennsylvania, a distance of 52 miles. Less clear is how it was built and when it began operating. The most likely date is 1838, although some accounts suggest as early as 1836. In either event, it was within the same decade as the first scheduled passenger train service in the United States.

Beginnings and Prosperity: 1867–1900

The car was the product of one of the leading railroad car designers of the time, Richard Imlay of Philadelphia. By the end of the decade, Imlay would also build bunk-style cars for the Philadelphia, Wilmington & Baltimore and Philadelphia & Columbia Railroads, both of which would become part of the great Pennsylvania Railroad.

But demand for overnight accommodations on the railroads of the 1830s was rather limited. Most operated over distances that could easily be covered in a day. Safe and practical nighttime operations would also have to await development of an effective oil- or kerosene-burning locomotive headlight lantern, a device that would not become widely accepted until the 1840s.

The earliest railway passenger cars often were designed and built by carriage-makers and, therefore, frequently had the appearance of being simply a carriage or stagecoach on flanged wheels. But railway technology, of course, permitted much larger carbodies to be placed on a single frame, especially after the introduction, in the mid-1830s, of independent, swiveling wheel assemblies or "trucks." The eight-wheel double truck soon replaced the four-wheel carriage design, thereby encouraging redesign of the carbody. By moving to essentially a rectangular box with an arched roof, carbuilders were able to increase carrying capacity and the flexibility of interior floor plans. It was now easier to install amenities such as water closets (restrooms in today's parlance) and stoves for heating. The addition of platforms and doors at each end of the car facilitated the employment of center-aisle interior designs, such as the alignment of transverse seats, one behind the other, on either side of the aisle. This also took advantage of the cars-in-tandem character of a train by letting passengers and crew members pass between the cars.

When overnight train travel became a reality, it was logical to fashion a nighttime equivalent to the daytime seat; that is, a place to lie down and sleep. Boats operating on the nation's canals and inland waterways generally had met this need with tiered bunk beds. Imlay's *Chambersburg* followed that precedent, but with the additional feature that the lower sleeping bunks were transformed from the upholstered seat cushions and backs of lengthwise day-seating benches set along the walls of the car. A third, top bunk folded down from the wall at a position below the ceiling. Both the day and night accommodations were pretty basic and were accompanied by few amenities. But they seemed to satisfy the needs of passengers traveling relatively short distances.

The proliferation and lengthening of rail lines in the 1840s and early 1850s, coupled with the modest success of Imlay's bunk cars, prompted a number of railroads, car builders and inventors to develop sleeping-car designs. Some sleepers were built new, others remodeled from coaches; but most were simply variations on the original two or three-tier bunk arrangement. Passengers, with assistance from trainmen, prepared the bunks for night use, drawing on bedding stored in lockers or topmost bunks. Few of these operations met with much success, due still in large measure to a lack of significant demand. The railroad map of 1850 remained comprised largely of short, independently operated routes, often of different gauges and relatively little inter-connectivity.

But things were changing. An all-rail route between Boston and New York had been achieved in 1848. Population and commercial centers were growing along waterways in the Midwest as well as in the Northeast and South, and the drive was on to connect them overland by rail lines. The first train entered Chicago from the East (Detroit) in 1852, the same year the Baltimore & Ohio Railroad linked tidewater Maryland with the Ohio River at Wheeling. Two years later, rails connected Chicago and St. Louis. Meanwhile, the recent discovery of gold in California was focusing attention on the West and how to exploit its resources. Just about everywhere in the newly burgeoning America, the situation was growing ripe for sleeping-car entrepreneurs.

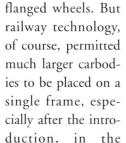
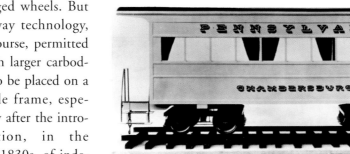

The first sleeping car is believed to have been the *Chambersburg,* introduced in the late 1830s on the Cumberland Valley Railroad, later a component of the Pennsylvania Railroad. Although the details of the design by carbuilder Richard Imlay are sketchy, this model is probably a reasonable replica of the car's exterior appearance. Seats were provided for day travel and tiered bunks gave passengers the option of lying down at night. *WILLIAM F. HOWES JR. COLLECTION*

Pullman's first sleeping cars were Chicago, Alton & St. Louis cars 9 and 19, which were remodeled at the railroad's shops in Bloomington, Illinois. Car 9 made its inaugural run from Bloomington to Chicago on the night of September 1, 1859, followed later in the year by No. 19. The two cars represented a modest, but welcome improvement in sleeping-car design. This view shows one of the cars on display at the 1948—49 Chicago Railroad Fair, decorated to represent service on Abraham Lincoln's funeral train. *GEORGE KRAMBLES, KRAMBLES-PETERSON ARCHIVE, JOE WELSH COLLECTION*

SLEEPING-CAR INVENTORS AND CONCESSIONAIRES

The first patent for a new sleeping car design went to Henry B. Myer in 1854. It involved modifying conventional day-coach seats so their backs could be pivoted into a position forming the upper of a two-tiered set of platforms that would run the length of the car. The lower platform was created from seat cushions hinged at the front so they could be flipped over and secured to fill the space between seats. Mattresses and bedding could then be placed anywhere along these platforms.

Of more lasting significance was a design patented in 1856 by Theodore Tuttle Woodruff, a master car builder on the Terre Haute, Alton & St Louis Railroad, another Pennsylvania Railroad precursor. This was the first to embrace the concept of a "section" comprising two convertible, facing seats that made up into two berths. A third berth was part of a hinged framework that folded down from the ceiling. Privacy was achieved by curtains hung in front of the berths. Woodruff's designs were employed by various car builders in sleeping cars

built for operation on the New York Central & Hudson River, Pennsylvania, and other roads beginning in 1858. Formed in 1857, T. T. Woodruff & Company was the first successful sleeping car company, establishing Woodruff as one of the pioneers in the operation of sleeping-car service as a concessionaire to the railroads.

Another pioneering sleeping-car designer and concessionaire of the period was Edward C. Knight, whose patents included several designs for an upper berth that dropped down from the ceiling. Knight's sleepers saw service in the early 1860s on the B&O, Camden & Amboy, and other railroads. In 1862, Knight and Woodruff consolidated their interests into the Central Transportation Company.

An 1859 patent by Eli Wheeler utilized Woodruff's section format, but designed the facing seat backs and cushions to pivot independently so as to come together to form a single lower berth. Some of Wheeler's ideas were later employed by George Pullman and others.

Webster Wagner, a former wagon-maker, was working as a station agent for the NYC&HR in 1858 when he

George Pullman was convinced that people would be attracted by, and willing to pay for, on-board amenities normally associated with a fine hotel. This car built for the Chicago & Alton incorporated Pullman's latest ideas. Details are sketchy, but the car was apparently somewhat taller and wider than normal in order to better accommodate Pullman's two-tiered section with its foldaway upper berth design. The car, designated "A" but later named *Pioneer*, established a new standard for luxurious appointments. Its cost, bloated by Civil War inflation and lavish decor, reached $20,000, considerably more than the typical railroad passenger car of the time. *THE PULLMAN COMPANY, KRAMBLES-PETERSON ARCHIVE, JOE WELSH COLLECTION*

RIGHT: *Mimas* was a 10-section drawing room-buffet car produced by the Pullman Car Works in 1884. The varnished upper berths featured one of Pullman's most popular marquetry patterns, "Pineapple." To create the pattern, figures of wood were cut from sheets of veneer and then glued to the berth fronts. Multiple hand-rubbed coats of varnish provided the finishing touch. Pullman interiors of the period featured such beautiful materials as rosewood, satinwood, amaranth and vermilion. *PULLMAN PHOTO, KRAMBLES-PETERSON ARCHIVE, JOE WELSH COLLECTION*

FAR RIGHT: Rudimentary but comfortable, open berths were offered on this tourist sleeper circa 1890. Facing lower seats form the lower berth, while the upper berth drops down from the ceiling. Patterned curtains are hung to provide a modicum of privacy. A clerestory window above provides both light and ventilation, and gas lighting fixtures hang from the ceiling. *PULLMAN PHOTO, KRAMBLES-PETERSON ARCHIVE, JOE WELSH COLLECTION*

secured a sleeping-car concession contract with Woodruff that led to the placing of Woodruff cars on the fast-expanding New York Central System. Over time, Wagner would draw upon his own and others' designs to build cars to operate on lines under the control of Central's Commodore Vanderbilt. One of Wagner's most important contributions was the introduction of a clerestory roof with adjustable shuttered vents that greatly improved ventilation, a major problem on early sleeping cars. Wagner formed the New York Central Sleeping Car Company in 1866.

As the Central's system expanded, Wagner's operations did likewise. With NYCS affiliate Lake Shore & Michigan Southern came Lake Shore's sleeping-car concessionaire, the Gates Sleeping Car Company, which had been operating cars on the LS&MS since 1858. The New York Central Sleeping Car Co. acquired Gates in 1869 and, in 1886, was renamed the Wagner Palace Car Company. Ironically, this happened four years after Wagner was killed in a collision on the New York Central.

Although less influential in the American sleeping car business than Woodruff, Knight, Wagner and Pullman, William D'Alton Mann also deserves mention as one of the pioneers in the field. Younger than the others, the flamboyant resident of Mobile, Alabama, did not enter the scene until 1871 when he embraced the European-style side-door compartment car. He settled in Europe and helped form Wagons-Lits, the International Sleeping Car Company—Europe's answer to The Pullman Company.

Returning to the United States in 1883, he established the Mann Boudoir-Car Company. Although Mann's cars were among the most lavish, and he finally adopted end-of-car entry, Mann's European-style shared compartments were not popular with Americans. Nevertheless, he did foresee before Pullman the public's interest in private room accommodations.

The story has it that George M. Pullman's first experience aboard a sleeping car was in 1853 on an overnight trip between Westfield and Buffalo, New York. Fully clothed, he tossed and turned uncomfortably on the narrow bunk and arrived fatigued. It was not a pleasant experience, but one that he would recall in the years ahead.

Born on March 31, 1831, in Brocton, New York, Pullman learned woodworking under his brother Albert's tutelage. While still in his early twenties, Pullman became skilled in the moving of buildings during the widening of the Erie Canal. He moved to Chicago in 1855 where he made a name for himself raising buildings, including the four-story all-brick Tremont House hotel, above the level of Lake Michigan as part of a massive downtown improvement project. When he returned to Brocton in 1857, he became reacquainted with Benjamin C. Field, a friend and former New York legislator. Field had previously acquired patents from T. T. Woodruff and was negotiating with the Chicago, Alton & St. Louis Railroad to remodel two of their coaches with sleeping accommodations.

CA&StL cars 9 and 19 were selected for remodeling, and the work was performed at the railroad's shops in Bloomington in central Illinois. Details of the construction are rather sketchy, but it is known that the cars had two tiers of berths versus the three common to most sleepers of the time. Positionable upper berths were installed and probably operated with ropes and counterweights. The backs of pairs of facing seats were hinged so that each seat back could be dropped to a horizontal position to form a lower berth. Bedding consisted of little more than a mattress and blankets. Car 9 made its inaugural run from Bloomington to Chicago on the night of September 1, 1859, followed later in the year by No. 19. The two cars represented a modest, but welcome improvement in sleeping-car design.

Pullman moved on to Colorado in 1860 where he was involved in the silver mining boom, including the sale and transportation of supplies for prospectors. When he returned to Chicago in 1863, he had money in his pockets and more ideas for improving the comfort of travel by rail. Field had added a third car on the CA&StL in 1861, but the Civil War had interrupted further development. However, Pullman envisioned a time after the war when expansion of the railroads westward would increase the need for sleeping cars. And, Pullman's vision went even further than that. He saw opportunities for an enterprise operating sleeping cars between cities without regard to the territorial limits of individual railroads. He believed a pool of cars was the most efficient way to handle localized surges in demand. And he was convinced that people would be attracted by, and willing to pay for, on-board amenities and luxuries normally associated with fine hotels of the period.

Pullman and Field contracted with the CA&StL—then recently renamed Chicago & Alton—to build a new car incorporating Pullman's latest ideas. Once again, details are sketchy, but the car was apparently somewhat taller and wider than normal in order to better accommodate Pullman's two-tiered section with its foldaway upper-berth design. The car, simply designated "A" but later named *Pioneer*, established a new standard for luxurious appointments. Its cost, bloated by Civil War inflation and lavish decor, reached $20,000, considerably more than the typical railroad passenger car of the time.

In the absence of photographs or detailed specifications for the original car, it's not surprising that its early years have become embroiled in mythology and controversy. For years, The Pullman Company suggested that its unconventional dimensions gained acceptance following the *Pioneer*'s last-minute assignment to the final leg—

A former Wagner Palace Car Company sleeper trails Chicago–Denver train No. 1 of the Chicago, Burlington & Quincy. Wagner became Pullman's chief competitor, but Pullman eventually ended the rivalry simply by buying out Wagner. *RAILWAY & LOCOMOTIVE HISTORICAL SOCIETY COLLECTION*

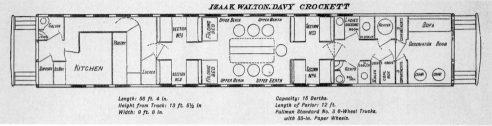

IZAAK WALTON. DAVY CROCKETT

Length: 56 ft. 4 In.
Height from Track: 13 ft. 5½ In.
Width: 9 ft. 8 In.

Capacity: 15 Berths.
Length of Parlor: 12 ft.
Pullman Standard No. 3 6-Wheel Trucks,
with 33-in. Paper Wheels.

TOP: Among the fascinating stable of cars that Pullman maintained for charter in the late 1800s were a few "hunting cars." Equipped with a kitchen, gun racks, dog kennels, and sleeping accommodations for parties of up to 15 people, cars *Izaak Walton* and *Davy Crockett* must have seen a lot of the Wild West before being retired near the turn of the twentieth century. Pictured here is the *Izaak Walton*. PULLMAN PHOTO, KRAMBLES-PETERSON ARCHIVE, JOE WELSH COLLECTION

RIGHT: Issued by Pullman in 1886, this interesting descriptive circular shows and explains the floor plans of cars (among them the *Izaak Walton* pictured above) that the firm maintained for charter to private parties. "Hotel" cars contained sleeping accommodations, a dining area and a kitchen. "Sleeping" cars offered up to 24 berths; "excursion" cars accommodated from 12 to 18 people offering a full bed for each as well as kitchen accommodations and an observation room. THE PULLMAN COMPANY, JOE WELSH COLLECTION

Chicago to Springfield, Illinois—of Abraham Lincoln's funeral train in 1865. Recent investigation suggests this story is fanciful. In any event, the *Pioneer* did contribute to a new chapter in the history of railroad passenger travel. It, and luxurious cars that followed, were heavily promoted by Pullman as examples of what was possible, what the public wanted, and what the public deserved.

GROWTH

The decade following the Civil War saw railroad mileage in the United States more than double from 35,085 in 1865 to 75,096 in 1875. The westward expansion had begun in earnest. Abraham Lincoln had recognized, even before the Civil War, the strategic importance of the railroad in the nation's growth and flow of interstate commerce. The war had further reinforced the railroads' role in uniting and defending the United States. The relatively well-developed system in the Northern states had clearly outperformed the less developed and loosely aligned railroads of the South. Whereas early railroads had been promoted largely at the state level, often as one state tried to gain a competitive edge over another, the focus was now on the need for a national network. Federal land grants would help push the rails westward. Standardization of track gauges would promote interline movement of

PULLMAN'S PALACE CAR COMPANY
Descriptive Circular
OF
HOTEL, SLEEPING, EXCURSION AND HUNTING CARS,
FOR
CHARTER TO SPECIAL PARTIES
WITH DIAGRAMS, RATES, ETC.

freight and passengers. Out of all this, George Pullman saw opportunity.

By 1867, Pullman owned 48 sleeping cars and had operating contracts with the Chicago & Alton, Michigan Central, Chicago, Burlington & Quincy, Chicago Great Western, and the Great Western Railway of Canada. That year he incorporated Pullman's Palace Car Company in Illinois and transferred his equipment assets and contracts to the new company. Shortly thereafter, the firm negotiated an operating contract with the Chicago & North Western.

Recognizing that comfortable day and overnight accommodations alone were not enough for a long trip, Pullman introduced the "Hotel Car" in 1867 by adding a small kitchen within the car for serving meals en route at one's seat. The first hotel car, the *President*, entered service on the Great Western Railway of Canada in 1867, followed shortly by the *Western World* and *Kalamazoo*. The next logical step was development of a car specifically for dining. Back in 1863, two day coaches on the Philadelphia, Wilmington & Baltimore had been modified to permit the serving of hot food prepared off the car and brought aboard. Pullman's approach was far more ambitious, involving nothing short of a luxurious full-service restaurant with kitchen and dining room on wheels. It was named, appropriately, the *Delmonico* after the famed restaurant and put in service on the C&A in 1868.

Next, Pullman expanded his operations into the market for luxury daytime travel with the introduction, in 1874, of parlor cars incorporating a saloon with deep-cushioned, reclining and revolving chairs. The car was based on a concept that Pullman had been using successfully on the Great Western Railway of Canada since 1871 and was currently introducing in Great Britain. It also followed in the footsteps of Webster Wagner and others who had been designing and operating first-class accommodations for day trips since the 1860s.

Pullman saw his sleeping, hotel, parlor, and dining cars as not just technological advances, but as components of a whole new level of service quality for a rapidly expanding travel market. It was not to be something solely for the wealthy. It would be designed to promote travel as well as to be a beneficiary of what he correctly believed to be the inevitable growth of the railroad network.

Early sleeping-car operations had often been staffed by the railroad's own employees or relied on passengers to prepare their own berths. By 1870, Pullman had decided to always staff his cars with his own conductors and porters. Taking advantage of the large pool of African-American labor that had become available upon Abraham Lincoln's freeing of the slaves, Pullman initially employed only black males for porter positions.

George Pullman was the consummate promoter for his business. Whether introducing his cars on the Chicago, Burlington & Quincy in 1866 with a tour between Chicago and Aurora; demonstrating the viability of interline Pullman operations on an 1867 excursion from Chicago to New York via Canada and, on the return trip, exposing Union Pacific president Thomas C. Durant to the potential for Pullman Palace Car service on his line; or hosting the Boston Board of Trade aboard eight elegant Pullman cars on the first transcontinental train from Boston to San Francisco in 1870, Pullman never missed an opportunity to press his vision of a nation linked by Pullman Palace Car lines and served by a pool of luxurious cars, expertly maintained and staffed.

BUILDING AND REPAIRING THE CARS

Pullman's early cars were built or remodeled at the shops of various railroads and car-building firms. However the success of his business and his intention to build passenger cars for others prompted him to acquire, in

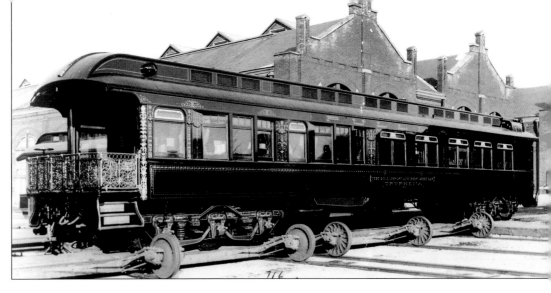

1870, the Detroit Car & Manufacturing Company and concentrate car construction there. As the decade progressed, and his dream for a national network of Palace Car cars lines was rapidly taking form, Pullman decided to build a new car works near the company's Chicago headquarters. It would be a state-of-the-art facility using the latest car-building technology. He chose a virgin site along the Illinois Central Railroad 15 miles south of downtown near Lake Calumet. Here he would not only build shops, but also a model town for his workers. The town of Pullman reflected its namesake's vision of an aesthetically attractive and well-ordered setting for management and labor alike, as well as his obsession with "standardizing" and controlling all elements of his business. The Pullman Car Works opened in 1881. In time, it was employing some 2,000 people, many immigrant craftsmen drawn to the attractive homes they could rent and the town's schools, libraries, and parks. By 1893,

Among the first in a long line of Pullman-built and operated section sleeper-observation lounge cars, the 1890 *Tryphene* (depicted here) and sister *Tryphosa* saw service on the Denver & Rio Grande and the Colorado Midland, including through-car operation between Denver and Salt Lake City. The 8 sections and observation-lounge of the wood cars were elaborately decorated with Pullman's finest marquetry. *GERALD M. BEST, CALIFORNIA STATE RAILROAD MUSEUM*

Wagner Vestibule composite (wood and steel) car No. 186 contained a baggage compartment and full-service buffet-lounge. The car was not included in Pullman's acquisition of the Wagner Palace Car Company, so it probably stayed in service somewhere on the New York Central System. *JOHN GIBB SMITH JR., RAILWAY & LOCOMOTIVE HISTORICAL SOCIETY COLLECTION*

Pullman Car Works on Chicago's far south side stands in elegant glory in this view that was probably taken shortly after the shop complex opened in 1881. The front of this portion of the works faced west and stood just east of Illinois Central's Chicago–New Orleans main line; the City of Pullman lay to the south (right in photo). Flanked by shop bays, the ornate headquarters building was still standing as of 2004 but had been heavily damaged by fire in the 1990s. The lagoon, with "Pullman" spelled out in white stone along the east bank, eventually gave way to a widened and elevated IC right-of-way as well as an extended Cottage Grove Avenue. The brick shop buildings show up in many a builder's photo (RIGHT, INSET) from the 1880s to the 1950s.—*THE PULLMAN COMPANY, ARTHUR D. DUBIN COLLECTION*

BELOW: *Wadena* was a narrow-vestibuled, 10-section 1-drawing-room stateroom car constructed in 1892 by the Pullman Car Works for the Pullman-Northern Pacific Association. Wood cars such as this required a significant amount of preparation and painting. After at least 18 days of prep, the first coat of the final color was applied. Depending on the shade of the final color, from two to four coats of final "flat" color were painstakingly applied. After the final coat and a day to dry, the car was turned over to the ornamenters. First applied using stencils and brush, the ornamentation was then shaded or gold leafed. Afterward, the car was varnished. All told, Palace Cars such as this sleeper could take up to 40 days to paint. Even the car's trucks have been painted with fine lining. *THE PULLMAN COMPANY, KRAMBLES-PETERSON ARCHIVE, JOE WELSH COLLECTION*

Pullman had a population of about 12,000 souls, but with the exception of its Hotel Florence, no bars—George Pullman wanted his employees to come to work sober. And this work had now expanded into new lines of car construction, including some freight-car orders.

But, Pullman's business philosophy was about to be sorely tested. An economic panic and depression in 1893 had cut deeply into the car-building business. In order to keep as many people employed as he could, he cut his workers' wages by nearly a third. Unfortunately, his refusal to make a commensurate reduction in home rents in the Town of Pullman and in his managers' salaries generated resentment—and the company's first serious, large-scale labor unrest.

Encouraged by Eugene V. Debs of the American Railway Union, the workers went on strike in May 1894 and, with the support of railroad labor, managed to bring many of the nation's trains to a standstill. The railroads turned to U.S. President Grover Cleveland for relief. Despite Debs's efforts to avoid violence, ugly battles erupted between the strikers, their sympathizers and Federal troops, the Illinois militia, and police. Twelve people died in the melee. Law enforcement prevailed, leaving Pullman's workers little to show for the effort. However, by rallying many to its cause, the event became a defining moment in the American labor movement.

The strike also appeared to break the spirit of George Pullman. He died three years later and was succeeded in the presidency by Robert Todd Lincoln, Pullman's general counsel and the son of Abraham Lincoln.

The depression and strike behind them, Pullman's Palace Car Company again prospered and continued its pursuit of a virtual monopoly in sleeping-car construction and operations.

To serve its expanding territory of operations, Pullman added repair shops at St. Louis (1880); Wilmington, Delaware (1886); Calumet, Illinois (1901); and Richmond, California (1909). Following the opening of

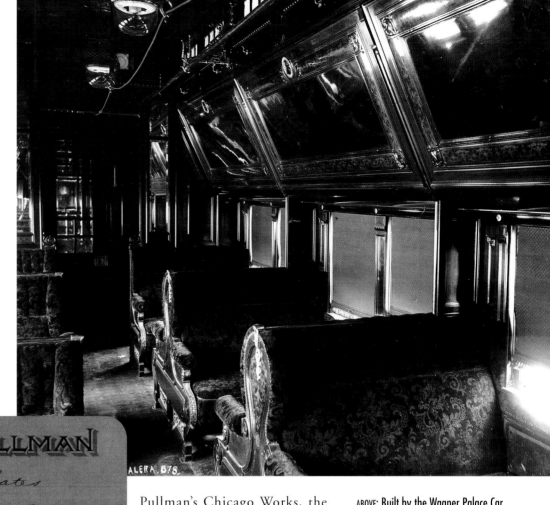

ABOVE: Built by the Wagner Palace Car Company in 1887, the *Glendale* contained 12 sections and 1 drawing room. The wood car was handsomely decorated in the style of the times. Following its acquisition of Wagner at the end of 1899, Pullman renamed the car *Calera* in 1901 to avoid confusion with an existing Pullman-Missouri Pacific Association car named *Glendale*. In common with many wood sleepers, the car was downgraded to tourist service in 1913 as Pullman tourist car No. 1517. *RAILWAY & LOCOMOTIVE HISTORICAL SOCIETY COLLECTION*

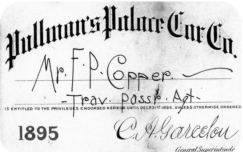

INSET: Passes allowed non-Pullman employees to travel gratis as a guest of The Pullman Company for a specified time. The upper pass dates from 1889; the lower from 1895. *JOE WELSH COLLECTION*

Pullman's Chicago Works, the Detroit Works was gradually converted from car building to a car-repair facility and, in 1902, sold. Newer repair shops were opened in St. Louis the following year. The acquisition of the Wagner Palace Car Company at the end of 1899 brought with it car shops at Buffalo, New York.

COMPETITION AND CONSOLIDATION

In addition to Pullman's growth in the years following the Civil War, a number of other sleeping-car companies were developing and growing and, in a few cases, giving Pullman stiff competition. Principal among these was Webster Wagner's New York Central Sleeping Car Company (renamed the Wagner Palace Car Company in 1886). Increasingly, the company was encroaching on Pullman "territory," such as the Michigan

An important part of Pullman's business during the late nineteenth century and first three decades of the twentieth was the chartering of private cars. One such car was the elegantly decorated *Iolanthe*, built by the company in 1888. Constructed of wood, the car's floor plan included two private staterooms, four open sections, a dining room and kitchen, and an observation lounge. It was withdrawn from charter service and sold in 1917 to the San Antonio, Uvalde & Gulf Railroad. *RAILWAY & LOCOMOTIVE HISTORICAL SOCIETY COLLECTION*

Central and Chicago & North Western. Wagner had become a formidable and contentious competitor and would, in fact, be the last sleeping-car concessionaire to capitulate to Pullman.

Another leading sleeping-car company of the period was the Central Transportation Company, organized in 1862 to consolidate the interests of T. T. Woodruff and Edward C. Knight. CTC had routes on several Eastern railroads and was probably the largest and strongest operator immediately following the Civil War. A subsidiary, the Southern Transportation Company, developed sleeping-car routes in the South after the war. In 1866, CTC inaugurated a fleet of particularly lavish Silver Palace Cars. Pullman and CTC competed vigorously for the sleeping-car concession on the first transcontinental railroad. With an assist from Andrew Carnegie, who had ties to CTC but had recently become impressed with George Pullman's ambition and business sense, Pullman succeeded in leasing Central Transportation in 1870, effectively eliminating it as a competitor.

Other companies included Crescent City Sleeping Car Company, which became Pullman Southern in 1871, and Jonah Woodruff's Sleeping & Parlor Coach Company which acquired the Lucas Sleeping Car Company of Atlanta in 1878 and, along with the Mann Boudoir Car Company, came under the control of the newly formed Union Palace Car Company in 1888. Pullman acquired Union in 1889.

Some companies, such as Pullman Pacific Car Company operating on the Union Pacific, were formed as a means of extending Pullman's reach into new, lucrative territories and were eventually absorbed into Pullman's Palace Car Company.

Not all railroads chose concessionaires to operate their sleeping-car and related services; some preferred to do it themselves. Notable among these were the Chicago, Milwaukee & St. Paul (The Milwaukee Road), the Great Northern, and the New York, New Haven & Hartford. As Pullman expanded its influence, all three of these roads did, eventually, contract with Pullman for service. In addition, some roads entered into an "association" arrangement with Pullman whereby the cars were held in joint ownership and car maintenance costs and profits were divided. This was a device that spread the initial investment cost and allowed Pullman to get a foothold on the railroad with respect to both the acquisition of equipment and the operation of the service. In most cases, Pullman eventually purchased the railroad's interest in the cars.

Despite widespread and spirited competition, by the mid-1880s Pullman was clearly the dominant player in the sleeping-car business. Competing companies were either folding or selling out to Pullman, with Wagner as the one significant exception. It took a bitter legal dispute over patents and operating contracts to finally prompt the Wagner Palace Car Company to yield to Pullman at the very end of 1899.

PULLMAN'S FOREIGN OPERATIONS

George Pullman's ambitions also went beyond the borders of the United States. As far back as 1867, Pullman had a contract with the Great Western Railway of Canada and introduced his Hotel Car service on the line. Although Pullman would never operate the local sleeping-car services of the Canadian Pacific, the company did run interline cars over that road, as well as both interline and some local Canadian services on lines which eventually became part of the Grand Trunk and Canadian National systems.

Pullman also developed a major presence in Mexico beginning in the 1880s. Its earliest recorded contract there was in 1884 with the Mexican Railroad. By the end of the decade, Pullman's Palace Cars were in regular service between the United States and Mexico. The first scheduled deluxe Pullman operation in Mexico was the tri-monthly, all-vestibule *Montezuma Special* inaugurated in late 1889 between New Orleans and Mexico City. Pullman initially operated and maintained its sleeping- and dining-car services in Mexico as districts of its U.S. operations, with employees used interchangeably between the two countries. By an action of the Mexican government in 1934, the movement of employees across the border was ended. Dining-car operations were taken over by the government-run railway in 1961, but Pullman continued as the sleeping-car concessionaire in Mexico until November 1970, nearly two years longer than in the United States.

Great Britain and continental Europe were also of interest to Pullman. In 1873, he contracted with the Midland Railway of Great Britain to provide sleeping cars of Pullman design modified to British specifications and to operate the service on the railway beginning in 1874. However, he discovered only a limited market for overnight sleepers, so he developed instead a luxury day trip service, including elegant on-board dining. The British Pullman Car Company was formed in 1882. Initially, it constructed cars at the Midland Railway's car works and the facilities of other railways, but eventually a Pullman car works was operated at Longhedge. Pullman cut its direct relationship with the British firm in 1906. Pullman's efforts to enter the market on the Continent ran into formidable competition from Mann's "Boudoir" compartment car and resistance from Wagons-Lits, so he never gained a foothold.

ADVANCING TECHNOLOGY

Pullman's history in the late nineteenth century was as much about technology as it was about business acumen. The 1880s saw a number of significant improvements in railroad car technology, including electric lighting, steam heat, and the enclosed vestibule. Pullman helped popularize many of them.

Electric lights: The glow of candles provided what little artificial light there was in the first railroad cars. By the 1840s kerosene- or whale-oil-burning lanterns had largely replaced the candles. Barely better than candles in providing light and often dirty and smelly, the lanterns were themselves replaced in the 1860s and 1870s by the Pintsch gas light, a widely-used lighting device developed in Germany. In 1882, just three years after Thomas Edison's invention of the incandescent light bulb, electric lighting was introduced on the Pennsylvania Railroad. Because its use not only enhanced car lighting but also reduced vulnerability to fire, its acceptance by the railroads was rapid, and by 1887 entire trains were advertised as being electric-lighted.

Steam heat: Wood and coal stoves on early rail cars toasted passengers in close proximity and left others shivering. The Baker Heater hot water system was introduced in 1865 and saw widespread use until the 1890s. In the mid-1880s, a practical way was found to efficiently send steam from the locomotive back through the train to heat cars in the consist, including for hot water and dining-car steam tables. This was modified to a low-pressure vapor system around 1910.

Vestibules: During railroading's first half century, passage between cars on a moving train had been risky at best and in bad weather downright dangerous and uncomfortable. Most passengers chose to stay put. Finally, in 1887, H. H. Sessions of the Pullman Company solved the problem with a vestibule incorporating a flexible enclosed passageway between cars. The device not only protected passengers from the elements, it controlled jarring and, by keeping adjoining platforms horizontally aligned, reduced the danger of the cars telescoping. The same year, the Pennsylvania Railroad's *Pennsylvania Limited* became the first fully vestibule-equipped train in America.

Pullman was quick to adopt these improvements. By

In 1907, The Pullman Company built its first all-steel sleeper, naming it *Jamestown* in recognition of the fact that it would be exhibiting the car at the upcoming Jamestown Exposition, which commemorated the first European settlement in America, in 1607 in today's Virginia. Pullman was responding to growing public pressure to replace wood cars, and their associate risks of fire and telescoping in accidents, with stronger, fire-resistant steel equipment. Carbuilders had already begun using steel for the underframe and vestibule construction to provide greater strength and facilitate the design of longer cars. Now, some railroads, such as the Pennsylvania with concerns about wood-car fires in the tunnels it was building in New York, advocated steel passenger cars. However, it would be three years before Pullman would convert to steel-car production. In the meantime, *Jamestown* was renamed *Talisman* after the exposition and then *Middletown* in 1911. It was removed from active service in 1943. *THE PULLMAN COMPANY, TRANSPORTATION COLLECTIONS, SMITHSONIAN COLLECTION*

the end of the century, most of the nation's premier trains would boast electric lights, steam heat, and vestibules.

NOTABLE TRAINS OF THE LATE NINETEENTH CENTURY

From the end of the Civil War until the 1880s, a number of sleeping-car service concessionaires, led by George Pullman and Webster Wagner, had vied for contracts to operate over the various railroads. Some railroads handled only the cars of one of the concessionaires. Other roads might have the services of two or more concessionaires or operate their own service plus that of a concessionaire. Having multiple operators was common when handling interline cars from a road aligned with a concessionaire different than your own. For an example, Wagner offered a Boston–St. Louis buffet-sleeping car that traversed the Fitchburg Railroad, a Pullman road, from Boston to Rotterdam Junction, New York; thence via the New York Central-controlled West Shore Railroad, a Wagner line, to Buffalo; and on to St. Louis in a train of the Wabash Railroad, which had both Pullman and Wagner local sleeping car lines. Passengers were more likely to relate to the concessionaire on whose car they were riding than to the particular train(s) or railroad(s) on which they were traveling.

Hotel-style cars made it possible to complete a trip without ever venturing into another car. Even where a separate dining car was operated on the train, passengers ventured across the open, weather-exposed space between cars warily and certainly no more often than necessary.

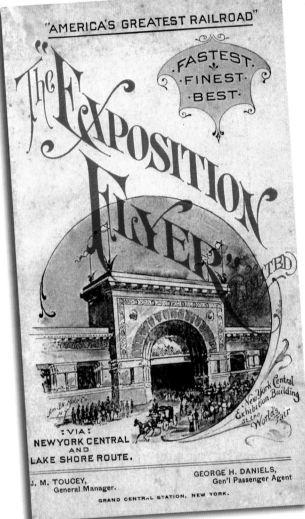

The *Exposition Flyer Limited* was operated on a blistering 20-hour schedule between New York and Chicago via the New York Central & Hudson River and affiliate Lake Shore & Michigan Southern in the summer and fall of 1893. Described by New York Central as "The Fastest Train on Earth," the *Flyer* carried passengers to Chicago's Columbian Exposition. Highly popular, the special train was removed from service at the conclusion of the Exposition, but its success inspired a series of future fast, regularly scheduled trains over the same route such as the *Lake Shore Limited* (1897) and the world's most famous train, the *20th Century Limited* (1902). The *Flyer* was equipped by Pullman's rival, Wagner. NYC, JOE WELSH COLLECTION

Interior of Dining Car

The Exposition Flyer

(LIMITED),

THE WORLD'S GREATEST TRAIN.

THE day of slow railway trains has passed, and a new era dawned in the history of transportation. Recognizing the demand for advanced railway service, meaning not only the latest conveniences of travel, but the highest speed attainable with safety, the New York Central, always in the van of progress, has been diligently experimenting with motive power and equipment, and is finally enabled to announce a triumphant solution of all problems encountered by the placing in service of the "EXPOSITION FLYER."

Sunday, May 28th, and thereafter every day in the year, this wonderful train will leave Grand Central Station, New York, at 3.00 p.m. (Eastern Time), and arrive in Chicago via the Lake Shore & Michigan Southern Railway at 10 o'clock (Central Time) the next morning, making the run in precisely twenty hours actual time.

But a few years ago the average running time between New York and Chicago was thirty-six hours; then the New York Central put on its famous "LIMITED," which made the run in twenty-four and three-quarter hours; next came the "EMPIRE STATE EXPRESS" with a record of a mile a minute, between New York and Buffalo, 440 miles, and finally the Exposition Flyer, reducing the time from New York to Chicago to twenty hours, and supplying the strongest link yet forged to unite the East and the West by facilitating the interchange of business between the two sections—undoubtedly entitled to rank among the greatest achievements of modern times. This is a record of progress matchless in conception, development and importance—worthy of 'AMERICA'S GREATEST RAILROAD."

The introduction of the enclosed vestibule beginning in 1887 greatly changed the rail travel experience. Now one could move safely and comfortably between cars, making it practical for the railroad or concessionaire to provide a variety of services and amenities elsewhere on the train. But to get the full benefit of the vestibule feature, as well as such other recent advances as steam heat and electric lighting, it was necessary to use only cars so-equipped in a train's consist. Thus, the "feature" train was introduced and promoted. It offered a variety of on-board services provided by a concessionaire, the railroad company, or both. Dining, club, and observation cars, libraries, barber shops, shower baths, maid-manicurists, and stenographers would soon be among the amenities advertised by the railroads for their premier runs. The traveler's attention would now be focused on what the entire train had to offer, not just the car he or she would occupy. As railroads realized the self-promotional possibilities of these trains, they gave them colorful, often self-identifying or even grandiose names and began performing some of the services, such as dining cars, themselves.

As public demand increased, many of what would become America's most famous trains were "born" in the years between 1887 and 1900, and most featured Pullman equipment. Among the notable new names found in railroad timetables as the century closed were *Pennsylvania Limited, Lake Shore Limited, Overland Limited, Sunset Limited, Fast Flying Virginian, New York & Florida Special, Pioneer Limited, North-Western Limited* and the Burlington Route's *Limited*.

Originally introduced in 1881 as the *New York & Chicago Limited*, the Pennsylvania Railroad's New York–Philadelphia–Chicago *Pennsylvania Limited* was renamed and inaugurated in 1887 as an extra-fare, all-

Buffet, Smoking and Library Car.

• The Route. •

THE physical and scenic advantages of the New York Central and Lake Shore Route are too well known to require detailed mention. Following the natural water way the entire distance from New York to Chicago, it encounters no steep grades or sharp curves, but has a perfectly straight track, seldom departing from a dead level, admitting the highest speed with absolute safety, and without any discomfort from vibration or oscillation.

From New York to Albany, a distance of 142 miles, it skirts the east shore of the historic Hudson River, then ascends the beautiful Mohawk Valley, traversing the cities of Schenectady, Utica, Rome, Syracuse, Rochester and Batavia to Buffalo—the Queen City of the Lakes. At Buffalo, uniting with the Lake Shore & Michigan Southern Railway, the route continues along the south shore of Lake Erie and Lake Michigan, traversing Pennsylvania, Ohio and Indiana, to Chicago, passing through the cities of Dunkirk, Erie, Cleveland, Toledo, Elkhart, South Bend and numerous other important commercial and manufacturing centres.

The Lake Shore & Michigan Southern Railway is a thoroughly built, finely equipped double track line, noted for its fine scenery and reliable service.

FOUR TRACKS.

Four tracks for the entire distance between Albany and Buffalo, over 300 miles, two devoted exclusively to passenger trains and two to freight, is a unique feature of the New York Central, and assures prompt service.

BLOCK SIGNALS.

The adoption by the New York Central of the latest and best system of interlocking block signals and switches, affords as perfect protection from accidents as human ingenuity can devise.

Interior of Sleeping Car.

Pullman vestibule train. The elegant stationery found at the writing desk in the library-smoking car hinted of the luxuries that defined this train, among them a ladies' private bathroom and maid, a stenographer, barber, periodic news and stock reports, and a dining car filled with steaks, oysters, and other culinary delicacies of the day. The train's sleeping accommodations included private drawing rooms and staterooms as well as open sections. Pullman's Palace Car Company updated the equipment in 1898 and the train was given an eye-catching color scheme of green beneath the window sash, yellow above the sash, and a red letterboard, prompting the nickname "Yellow Kid." But the *Pennsylvania Limited* was just a precursor of the luxury that would come to the PRR's New York–Philadelphia–Pittsburgh–Chicago run with the introduction of the *Pennsylvania Special* and *Broadway Limited* early in the next century.

The *Lake Shore Limited* of Commodore Vanderbilt's New York Central System was the *Pennsylvania Limited*'s chief competitor linking Chicago and New York. And the Wagner Palace Car Company that equipped and operated services on that train was Pullman's last major competitor. The *Lake Shore's* consist, which included a sleeper from Boston added at Albany, boasted vestibules, electric lighting, private room accommodations, and service amenities comparable to the *Pennsylvania Limited*.

Deluxe winter-season service was initiated in January 1888 with the all-Pullman *New York & Florida Special* running tri-weekly on a 30-hour schedule between New York and Jacksonville over 1,074-miles of the Pennsylvania; Richmond, Fredericksburg & Potomac; Atlantic Coast Line and Plant System railroads. The train was equipped with vestibuled sleepers, library-buffet car, dining and observation cars, all lighted by electricity from a dynamo in the baggage compartment and heated by steam from the locomotive. The train was soon extended over Henry M. Flagler's Florida East Coast to carry passengers directly to his Ponce de Leon Hotel at St. Augustine.

PULLMAN·VESTIBULE·TRAIN

SLEEPING CAR
The Pennsylvania Limited.

DINING CAR
The Pennsylvania Limited.

SMOKING CAR AND LIBRARY
The Pennsylvania Limited.

The Pennsylvania Limited.

Connecting New York, Philadelphia, and Washington with the posh resorts at Hot Springs, Virginia, and White Sulphur Springs, West Virginia, and beyond to Cincinnati was the *Fast Flying Virginian* (*FFV*) of the Chesapeake & Ohio Railway and Pennsylvania Railroad. Inaugurated in 1889, two train sets of seven cars each were built by Pullman and incorporated vestibules, electric lighting, and steam heat. The *FFV* introduced C&O's new orange-with-maroon-letterboard color scheme and was the road's first train to provide dining-car service. In addition to room and berth accommodations in Pullman's Palace cars, the train offered deluxe coach seating.

Two of Pullman's finest services in the West were the *Overland Limited*—jointly operated by the C&NW, Union Pacific, and Southern Pacific between Chicago and Kansas City and San Francisco—and SP's *Sunset Limited* linking San Francisco, Los Angeles, and New Orleans. The *Overland Limited* name did not appear on the through service of train Nos. 1 and 2 until 1899, but UP had used the name since 1896 when it replaced *Overland Flyer* which, in turn, dated from 1887. Although SP's predecessor, Central Pacific, had once operated its own Silver Palace sleeping

ABOVE: An 1889 brochure for the *Pennsylvania Limited* touts the advantages of this "Pullman Vestibule Train." A Pullman dining car, sleeping cars, and library-smoking car were offered. Among the novel features of the *Limited* were a barber and bath. *JOE WELSH COLLECTION*

LEFT: Ornate dining rooms were found in many of the cars Pullman maintained for private charters. The *Rambler* had two open sections immediately adjacent to its dining room and two private bedrooms toward the rear of the car. Built in 1885 for Richard Blanchard as the *Le Paradis*, the car was not delivered, but instead retained as a Pullman private car named *Glen Eyre*. In 1899, it was renamed *Rambler* and sold four years later to the San Pedro, Los Angeles & Salt Lake Railroad. *RAILWAY & LOCOMOTIVE HISTORICAL SOCIETY COLLECTION*

cars, first-class and tourist sleepers on the *Overland Limited* were a vestibule-equipped Pullman operation, with amenities such as a buffet-library car. The *Overland* also carried coaches with reclining seats.

The *Sunset Limited* dated from 1894 when a five-car first-class train of Pullman-built, vestibule-equipped wood cars began operating once a week between California and New Orleans. Occupants of Pullman's Palace Car sleepers had at their disposal a barber shop and bath in the combination buffet-baggage car and Southern-style meals in the diner, such as oysters, shrimp, biscuits, and corn cakes for breakfast.

Evidence that sleeping-car competition existed in the late 1890s and produced extraordinary service could be found in the overnight trains of the CM&StP, C&NW, and the CB&Q between Chicago and the Twin Cities of Minneapolis and St. Paul.

The Milwaukee owned and operated the sleeping, buffet, and dining car on its *Pioneer Limited*, and they were as fine as anything available from Pullman or Wagner. The *Pioneer* name debuted in 1898 when nameless train Nos. 1 and 4 were upgraded with sleepers, coaches, library-buffet cars and diners built by Barney & Smith of Dayton, Ohio, and Harlan & Hollingsworth of Wilmington, Delaware. Fully vestibule equipped and electrically lighted, the *Pioneer*—so named because the Milwaukee was first to launch through passenger service between Chicago and St. Paul—was notable for it rich interior woodwork.

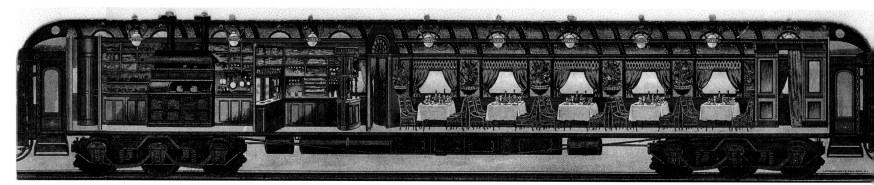

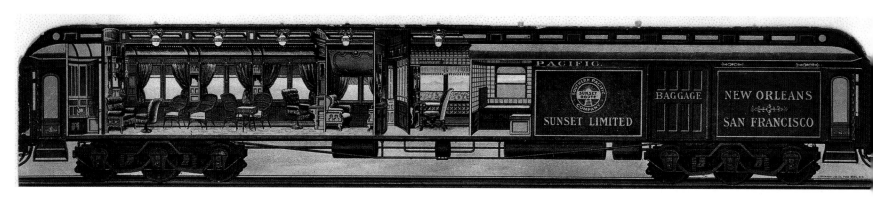

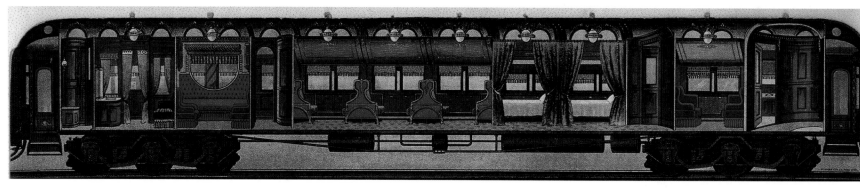

Also in 1898, the Buffalo Shops of Wagner Palace Car Company built vestibule-equipped, electrically lighted cars for the C&NW's *North-Western Limited*. Typically, Wagner employed mahogany, walnut, and other woods, plus costly fabrics to decorate the cars' interiors. Unusual in this market, the train's overnight coaches had reclining seats.

The *St. Paul Pioneer Press* called the Burlington Route's 1897 *Limited* the "finest regular train on earth." And that may have been true. Certainly, Pullman and the Burlington went all out to make sure this train exceeded those of its rivals on the Chicago–Minneapolis run. The two, five-car consists were vestibule-equipped and provided lighting by both Pintsch gas and electricity. The woodwork, with marquetry throughout the sleepers and library-buffet car,

was especially beautiful. Coach passengers had the convenience of larger-than-normal washrooms.

As the Pullman's Palace Car Company changed its name to The Pullman Company and absorbed the Wagner Palace Car Company in the first days of the twentieth century, its officers surely must have marveled at how far the firm had come in just over 30 years. Many challenges lay ahead—including growing pressure to strengthen the fleet with steel construction—but in less than three decades it could be said that George Pullman had successfully defined the American sleeping-car market and how to turn a profit from it. In the process, Pullman achieved a virtual monopoly in the building and operation of sleeping cars in the United States.

Inaugurated in 1894, the Southern Pacific's long lived *Sunset Limited*—it still operates today under Amtrak—originally ran between San Francisco and New Orleans. It underwent many equipment changes in its life. It's safe to say that perhaps the most elegant equipment ever operated on the train was that used before the turn of the twentieth century. In 1896 SP produced a magnificent die-cut brochure to promote the *Sunset*. It offered color cutaway views of the train's Pullman sleeping cars including its 10-section 2-drawing room cars and its "Ladies Combined Parlor and Compartment Car" with seven staterooms and a parlor complete with library and writing desk. *SP, JIM BECKWITH COLLECTION*

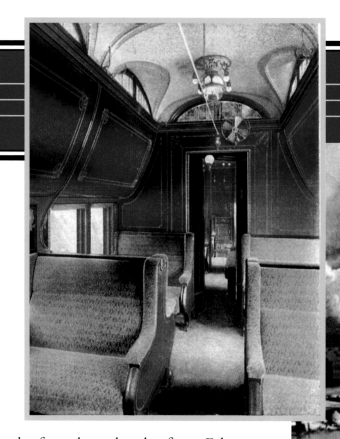

In the four short decades from February 1867, when George Pullman's company was organized, to March 1907, when it built its first steel car, Pullman grew from an obscure business enterprise to an American institution. Due to increasing demand for its service, in the early 1880s Pullman built a massive car manufacturing plant and model community—America's first planned community—for its employees in the new town of Pullman, Illinois, 15 miles south of downtown Chicago. Ironically, however, labor unrest—in part due to Pullman's near total control of the lives of its workers—would be the company's biggest problem in the last decade of the century. The divisive Pullman Strike of 1894 would subject the company to nationwide scrutiny and scorn, contributing to the death (by heart attack) in 1897 of the company's founder and patriarch George M. Pullman.

Despite the strike, Pullman's future as a company was ensured by the steady rise in influence (and mileage) of the American railroad. Total American railroad mileage expanded from 39,000 miles to 229,000 miles between 1867 and 1907. The railroads had virtually

text continued on page 40

RIGHT: An attractive young woman is assisted aboard the observation car of the *Los Angeles Limited*. When inaugurated on its Chicago—"City of Angels" run in 1905, the lavishly appointed consist was promoted as "a palatial train for particular people." The mahogany-paneled smoking room in the observation car was a popular gathering spot for gentlemen and liberated women during the transcontinental journey over the rails of the Chicago & North Western, Union Pacific, and San Pedro, Los Angeles & Salt Lake. Note the unusual, oversize rear window. *CALIFORNIA STATE RAILROAD MUSEUM, UNION PACIFIC COLLECTION*

BELOW: Inaugurated in December 1905, the *Los Angeles Limited* operated between Chicago and Los Angeles on the Chicago & North Western, Union Pacific, and the Salt Lake Route. The train offered passengers a relaxed atmosphere on the roughly 70-hour journey. By day, views of the unspoiled American West were available from the brass-railed observation platform or the enclosed observation room (FAR RIGHT). At night there was plenty of time for a good book in your berth or a smoke in the lounge for gentlemen. The train is shown in Palisade Canyon, Nevada, in the 1900s.—*UNION PACIFIC RAILROAD MUSEUM, JOE WELSH COLLECTION*

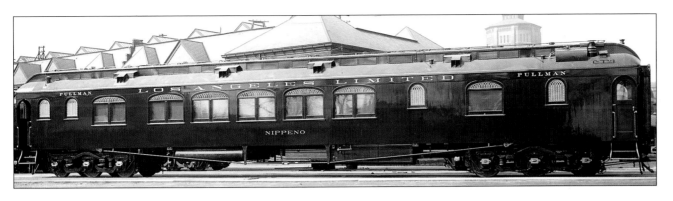

LEFT: Built in 1907, *Nippeno* was one of ten, 10-section 1-drawing room 2-compartment sleepers built for the *Los Angeles Limited* (see accompanying floor plan). With a wide vestibule and beautifully arched windows, the car was a classic example of a late wood-era Pullman car produced between 1905 and 1910. *PULLMAN, KRAMBLES-PETERSON ARCHIVE, JOE WELSH COLLECTION*

LEFT: The Maopa, a 10-section 1-drawing-room 2-compartment car decked out in Pullman green with gold-leaf lettering, was built by Pullman in 1906 for service on the *Los Angeles Limited*. The posh service between Chicago and Los Angeles had been inaugurated a year earlier. Constructed of wood, the car was eventually given a steel underframe and vestibules. It was scrapped in 1931. *RAILWAY & LOCOMOTIVE HISTORICAL SOCIETY COLLECTION*

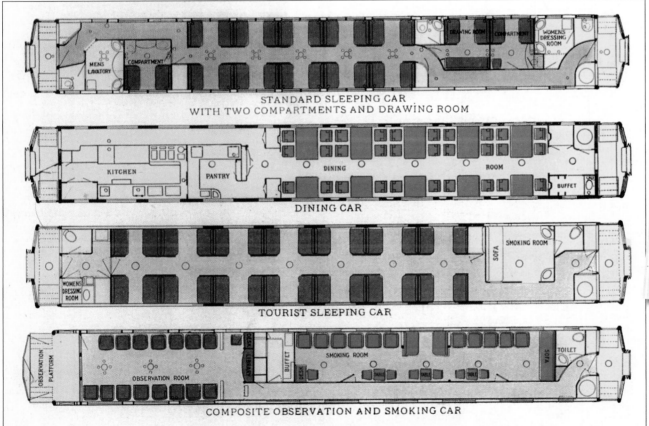

STANDARD SLEEPING CAR
WITH TWO COMPARTMENTS AND DRAWING ROOM

DINING CAR

TOURIST SLEEPING CAR

COMPOSITE OBSERVATION AND SMOKING CAR

The Los Angeles Limited
EVERY DAY IN THE YEAR

between
CHICAGO
AND
SOUTHERN CALIFORNIA
ELECTRIC LIGHTED

LEFT AND ABOVE: This stunning color brochure for the *Los Angeles Limited* issued circa 1907 shows the interior of one of the train's standard sleepers as well as the floor plans of its cars. *UNION PACIFIC, JIM BECKWITH COLLECTION*

39

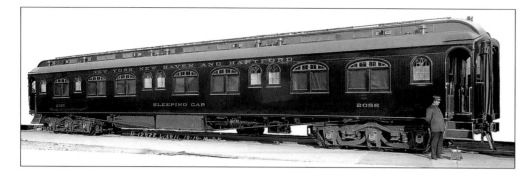

Although the New York, New Haven & Hartford owned and operated its own sleeping and parlor cars well into the twentieth century, many of its cars were built by Pullman. Such was the case with 16-section sleeper 2032 built in 1903. The wood carbody rode on a steel underframe; vestibules were also steel. This car was among the New Haven's assets acquired by Pullman in 1912. Pullman named the car *Gaetina*. It was scrapped in 1932.—*RAILWAY & LOCOMOTIVE HISTORICAL SOCIETY COLLECTION*

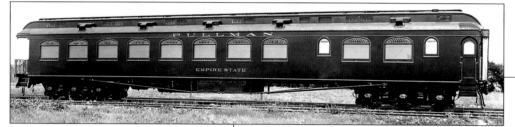

UPPER: Pullman constructed the 16-section sleeper *Boston* in 1903 for service on the Boston & Albany, once a Wagner road. Renamed *Nemeha* in 1914, the car's wood construction prompted its assignment to tourist-car service four years later as No. 4144. *RAILWAY & LOCOMOTIVE HISTORICAL SOCIETY COLLECTION*

ABOVE: Three wooden parlor-observation cars— *Buffalo, New York,* and *Empire State*—were built by Pullman in 1908 for assignment to the New York Central System's famed *Empire State Express* operating between New York City and Buffalo. Accommodations included 27 rotating easy chairs and a private drawing room. Although built of wood, the cars eventually received steel underframes and side sheathing. The *Empire State* was renamed *Pablo* in 1912, *Winifred* in 1924, and sold to the Tennessee Central in 1942. *RAILWAY & LOCOMOTIVE HISTORICAL SOCIETY COLLECTION*

text continued from page 36

no competition. As the railroads grew, so did Pullman's business, and Pullman enjoyed a near monopoly in the sleeping-car business, controlling almost 90 percent of the railroad sleeping-car service in North America.

This massive corporation was so rich in cash that it paid out regular, large stock dividends and easily absorbed its principal remaining rival, the Wagner Palace Car Company, in 1899. The price tag for Wagner was a whopping $36 million. At the start of the new century in 1900, Pullman officially renamed itself from the Pullman's Palace Car Company to simply The Pullman Company. The new name better fit Pullman's image in the twentieth century—a stately, no-nonsense institution.

The first decade of the new century would be the best in Pullman's history. Between 1900 and 1910 the company's traffic tripled and its assets doubled. Pullman's profits peaked in 1910. The company had no funded debt, and its net earnings on operations were over $13 million annually. By then, Pullman's cars reached the shores of the Atlantic and Pacific oceans, the Gulf of Mexico, and the far reaches of Canada and Mexico.

Pullman helped make American railroads into the finest land transport in the world. Since the 1880s Americans had been obsessed with the fast, first-class travel embodied by

the "Limited" train, so named for the limited stops it made. Many great "name trains" were added to the railroad scene in first decade of the twentieth century, among them the (appropriately named) *20th Century Limited* (1902) over the New York Central System between New York and Chicago; its great rival, the *Broadway Limited* (1902, initially named the *Pennsylvania Special*) via the Pennsylvania Railroad; the *North Coast Limited* (1900) between St. Paul and Seattle via the Northern Pacific Railroad; and the *Los Angeles Limited* (1905) between Chicago and Los Angeles via the Chicago & North Western and Union Pacific. Pullman was a key component of all of the trains listed above as well as many other trains of the era, offering exquisitely furnished sleeping, lounge, or parlor cars, personal service, and a host of other perks such as refined meals that helped distinguished the trains as the best travel experience that money could buy.

THE STEEL CAR ERA

As Pullman reached the pinnacle of its success, it also underwent a radical shift in the way it handled its passengers. For decades, the wooden railroad car had been the standard of American passenger carriage. But the world was changing. New York's pioneering Interborough Rapid

ABOVE: The steel framing for Pullman's first production line, all-steel sleeper, the Carnegie, completed in June 1910. *SMITHSONIAN INSTITUTION, WILLIAM F. HOWES JR. COLLECTION*

LEFT: Following the 1907 construction of the first all-steel sleeper *Jamestown*, to demonstrate the technology, Pullman began its production of steel sleeping cars in 1910 with the 12-section 1-drawing-room *Carnegie* for operation on the Pennsylvania Railroad. Before the year was out, another 300 steel 12-1 sleepers would be built for assignment on the PRR in response to that road's determination to operate only steel cars through the tunnels into its new Manhattan terminal, Pennsylvania Station. *SMITHSONIAN INSTITUTION, WILLIAM F. HOWES JR. COLLECTION*

The Tourist Sleeping Car

PICTURE a sleeping car with a decorative treatment unlike any thing heretofore attempted. The principal color employed is a soft restful gray green with furnishings in complementary tones and shades producing an effect of quiet restfulness that is satisfying and unique. Permanent partitions between the sections are carried to and across the ceiling in a series of charming colonnades.

NOT everyone can afford *all* the luxuries of modern travel hence the tourist sleeping car affording a maximum of travel comfort without frills and luxuries and at a minimum cost. The Oriental's tourist cars set a new mark for accommodations of this class. They are devoid of the decorative finish and the permanent headboards between sections that distinguish the other sleeping cars and the well cushioned seats are upholstered in leather instead of plush.

ABOVE AND FACING PAGE: A 1920s-era brochure for the *Oriental Limited* featured a stylish woman in cloche hat and knee-length skirt waving *adieu* as she passed through a fanciful iron train gate toward the train's bold, crimson tail sign. The Roaring Twenties would be the pinnacle for rail travel in terms of number of passengers carried.—*GN, JOE WELSH COLLECTION*

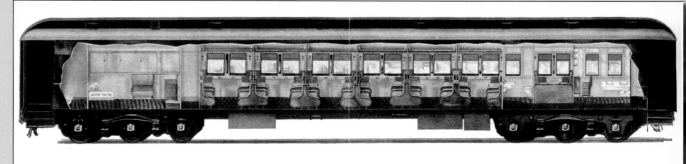

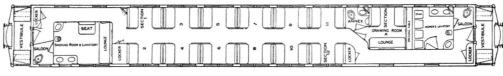

Cut out and plans of Twelve Section One Drawing Room Standard Pullman Sleeping Car showing roomy dressing rooms for both sexes and details of car's convenient arrangement.

Transit subway cars of the early 1900s were of steel construction to reduce the risk of fire, especially in tunnels. Interborough's neighbor, the giant Pennsylvania Railroad, which had been tunneling under the Hudson River in an ambitious project to put a passenger station in the heart of Manhattan, likewise focused on a changeover to steel rolling stock. Soon, an increasing number of roads took notice. By 1906, Pullman management decided to proceed with the development of steel cars. Pullman's first experimental steel car, the 12-section 1-drawing room sleeper *Jamestown* outshopped in March 1907, was exhibited at the Master Car Builders' Convention. Well built,

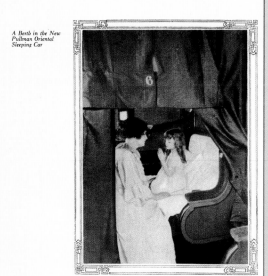

A Berth in the New Pullman Oriental Sleeping Car

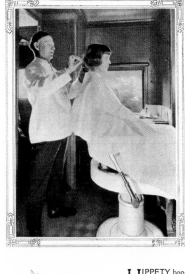

The Barber Shop

The Women's Shower Bath—A Travel Innovation

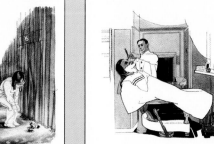

IT is in its extra large, extra restful sleeping car berths that the Oriental Limited reaches its highest point of comfort. Contributions to this include practically sound proof sleepers, the new permanent headboards, individual ventilators, reading lights in both upper and lower berths, clothes hangers, concealed floor lights, electric call bells and many other innovations and conveniences.

HIPPETY hop to the barber shop runs the old Mother Goose rhyme and here it is just forward of the dining car. The shop is in charge of a skilled white barber of long experience and here you may obtain all of the ministrations common to barber shops everywhere at reasonable prices. Milady may even have her hair bobbed enroute if she wishes. The barber shop also carries a complete line of toilet necessities for sale.

THE modern and up-to-date woman has added to her repertoire of hygienic features and her daily toilette is no longer complete without the refreshing "shower" bath. Sensing that this feature would prove particularly acceptable on a transcontinental trip the Oriental's builders provided a place for it just off the women's lounge room.

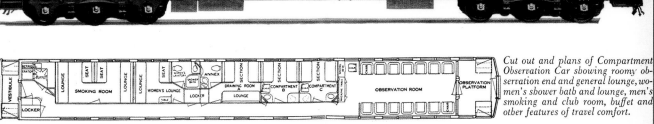

Cut out and plans of Compartment Observation Car showing roomy observation end and general lounge, women's shower bath and lounge, men's smoking and club room, buffet and other features of travel comfort.

LEFT: Eight cars in the *Great* series were constructed in May 1924 for the *Oriental Limited*. A ninth car was delivered in June 1926. GREAT NORTHERN, *JOE WELSH COLLECTION*

but very heavy at 81 tons, the *Jamestown* contributed to Pullman's efforts to perfect the steel car. A second prototype, the *Carnegie*, built for assignment to the Pennsylvania Railroad, was completed in 1910. Weighing in at 68 tons, it lessened the weight problem while proving durable and safe.

Pullman never looked back and committed to converting to steel cars immediately—a massive undertaking. No new wooden Pullman cars were built after 1910. By 1913, 2,100 all-steel sleeping cars (a third of Pullman's fleet) were in operation. In addition, 600 wood cars had been rebuilt with all-steel underframes.

Crossing the Missoula River near Bonner, Montana, Northern Pacific's *North Coast Limited* makes a fine portrait of varnish in the American West in the 1920s and 1930s. Direct competitor to GN's *Oriental Limited* and later the *Empire Builder* as well as Milwaukee Road's *Olympian*, the *North Coast* was an all-Pullman train on a three-night-out schedule between Chicago and Puget Sound. *NORTHERN PACIFIC, JIM BECKWITH COLLECTION; BROCHURE, JOE WELSH COLLECTION*

GROWTH, REGULATION AND GOVERNMENT CONTROL

Pullman continued to grow as an integral part of the expansion of America's railroads while yet more exotic name trains were introduced, many offering Pullman service. One of these would arguably be the most exclusive and luxurious American train of all time, Santa Fe Railway's *de-Luxe*. Running on a once-a-week schedule between Chicago and Los Angeles, the winter-season-only train began operation in December 1911. Interiors of its new Pullman sleeping cars boasted rosewood and mahogany trim. Patronage for the entire train was limited to just 60 passengers who paid a then-princely sum of $25 extra fare (in addition to a $46 fee for a drawing room). Each run was memorable for the amenities offered on board such as a barber, ladies' maid, and stenographer as well as for the speed of the journey: a scorching 63 hours—at that time the fastest travel time ever between Chicago and Los Angeles. Meals were provided by the legendary Fred Harvey in a dining car with a unique air washing/cooling

North Coast Limited

Pullmans Only—No Extra Fare

device that preceded true air-conditioning on American railroads by two decades. Sadly, the seasonal train's career would be cut short by World War I.

The *de-Luxe*, with its all-drawing-room or compartment cars, represented the epitome of American long-distance travel in its day, but Pullman's bread and butter were the thousands of less-exotic trains in service nationwide. Operating a massive fleet of sleeping cars, it relied on standardization to control costs and manage its business. This was most evident in the company's reliance on standard floor plans. Between 1907 and 1931—the last year a new heavyweight standard sleeper was built by Pullman and perpetuating a set of accommodations that had existed from the early days of the wooden car era—over 4,000 12-section 1-drawing room cars were built—half of all the sleeping cars completed in the period. The dark green, steel cars could be found in every nook and cranny of America from Maine to Los Angeles and Seattle to Key West. The Pullman section accommodation, with its distinctive heavy green curtains providing a modicum of privacy at night, became a part of American culture in the first half of the twentieth century, being featured in Hollywood movies, incorporated in the plots of novels and tolerated, praised, or vilified by the average traveler, depending upon his experiences with it.

Pullman itself became a part of the common American experience as it expanded its empire. Eventually, this drew the attention of the public and the government in a less-than-favorable way when the sleeping-car giant was accused of charging high prices and amassing huge prof-

With the **Indian Chiefs** on the **NORTH COAST LIMITED**

its. At the instigation of Congress, Pullman came under the regulation of the Interstate Commerce Commission (ICC) in 1906. Pullman lawyers fought a rearguard action against the government, but in 1910 Pullman finally began reporting its affairs to the ICC. The regulation had little effect on Pullman's expansion. In 1912 Pullman absorbed the sleeping-car fleet of the New York, New Haven & Hartford Railroad.

But America's entrance into World War I temporarily halted Pullman's directing of its own business. In 1918, Pullman's operations (but not manufacturing) were taken over by the United States Railroad Administration, which was responsible for managing most of the nation's railroads due to the war emergency. For the price of $11.75 million per year, the government essentially rented the Pullman Company and its personnel. It moved millions during the crisis.

BOOM TIMES—THE 1920S

Control of Pullman was returned to the company in March 1920. At year's end, Pullman owned a total of 7,726 cars including 5,751 regular sleeping cars, 808 tourist (no frills) sleepers, 1,019 parlor cars, 117 composite cars, 27 private cars (available for charter), and four miscellaneous cars. The company also leased another 26 cars from a handful of railroads for operation. Absent were full dining cars, which Pullman once operated for several railroads. Of these cars, 4,234 were of steel construction. Pullman also had another 87 parlor cars rented by the Pennsylvania Railroad and listed as not being in the service of Pullman.

ABOVE: Beginning in 1930, the *North Coast Limited* was assigned Pullmans with 10 sections, 1 drawing room, and 1 compartment. Appropriate for a train that traversed the American West, the cars were named in the *Chief* prefix series. *Chief Many Horns* served in long-term assignment to the NP which eventually purchased the car with the break-up of Pullman and leased it back to the company for operation. Here, the car is pictured painted in NP's postwar two-tone green "pine tree" scheme. The car was withdrawn from Pullman lease in 1954 and became a dormitory car.—*W. C. WHITTAKER, JOE WELSH COLLECTION*

LEFT: NP issued a brochure outlining the historical connection between its *Chief*-series Pullman cars and the Native American leaders for which they were named. *JOE WELSH COLLECTION*

In 1920 Pullman was a giant enterprise employing 22,886 people including 5,641 employees involved in maintenance, 15,971 people working in operations (including 2,430 conductors, 7,242 porters and maids), 4,617 car cleaners and even four train stenographers (used on premier trains such as the *20th Century Limited*). Its auxiliary operations included 168 commissary agents, staff conductors, waiters, cooks, and related. General-expense positions included its 34 general officers and 1,049 clerks and attendants.

The fact that the company engaged over 10,200 employees in maintenance and cleaning and over 1,000 clerks to keep track of everything reveals what a labor-intensive business Pullman was running. Pullman was essentially a giant hotel company whose 175,000 accommodations and thousands of patrons and staff started the

AERIAL PERSPECTIVE DRAWING OF CLUB CAR

NOTE: ROOF AND UPPER HALF OF NEAR SIDE OF CAR REMOVED TO SHOW INTERIOR ARRANGEMENT · BUILT BY PULLMAN CO · 1930 · OVERALL LENGTH 84 FT. · ⓛ=LOCKER Ⓦ=WARDROBE Ⓣ=TOILET Ⓘ=ICE Ⓡ=REFRIGERATOR ⓢⓕ=SODA FOUNTAIN

LEFT: Pullman baggage-club cars offered the equivalent of a gentlemen's club where men could enjoy a good cigar and good masculine conversation without the worry of offending delicate ears back in the observation car. In this 1920s view, an all-male group of passengers is attended to in a baggage-club car assigned to the legendary *20th Century Limited.*— BOB'S PHOTO; BROCHURE, JOE WELSH COLLECTION

TWENTIETH CENTURY LIMITED

Standard Bearer of NEW YORK CENTRAL SERVICE

Along the HUDSON RIVER by Daylight

NEW YORK CENTRAL LINES

evening in one city and state and ended it in another. Managing Pullman was perhaps the world's biggest chess game. Pullman's Car Service Department at headquarters received reports of each car's location every day. Cars had to be inspected and serviced— or "turned"—to be ready for the next trip. Inevitably some cars required unexpected maintenance and had to be replaced on short notice. The average Pullman car traveled 136,000 miles a year and visited numerous terminals, so keeping track of the fleet was no minor matter—and it was all done without computers.

And Pullman was about to get much busier. The economic boom and the associated growth in travel of the 1920s would result in the addition of hundreds of new trains and thousands of Pullman cars nationwide. The Pennsylvania Railroad, one of the nation's largest carriers, added a host of new limiteds in the period including the *Rainbow* and the *Golden Arrow* between New York and Chicago, the *Liberty Limited* between Washington and Chicago, the *Spirit of St. Louis* between New York/Washington and St. Louis, the

47

Cincinnati Limited between New York and Cincinnati and the *Pittsburgher* linking New York and Pittsburgh. All offered Pullman service.

The period saw the introduction of other new name trains by their principal sponsor roads such as the Cincinnati–New Orleans *Pan-American* (Louisville & Nashville, 1921), the Chicago–Washington–Jersey City *Capitol Limited* (Baltimore & Ohio, 1923), the New York–Miami *Orange Blossom Special* (Seaboard Air Line, 1925), the New York–New Orleans *Crescent Limited* (Southern Railway, 1925), the Chicago–Los Angeles *Chief* (Santa Fe, 1926), and the Chicago–Seattle/Portland *Empire Builder* (Great Northern, 1929). Railroads also chose to significantly refurbish their existing trains to stay competitive. Among the outstanding examples of these were the Chicago–St. Louis *Alton Limited* (Chicago & Alton, 1924) and the Chicago–Tacoma, Washington, *Olympian* (The Milwaukee Road, 1927). Pullman played a major role in all of these and many more, manufacturing much of their equipment and operating the first-class services on the trains.

Pullman absorbed almost all the remaining independent sleeping- and parlor-car operations in America in the 1920s. GN joined Pullman in 1922; in 1925 regional carrier Central of Georgia came aboard; and in 1927 the financially strapped Milwaukee Road (the last of the major holdouts) transferred most of its sleeping-car service to Pullman, benefiting from the influx of new Pullman equipment it couldn't have afforded otherwise. By the late 1920s, Pullman operated 97 percent of the sleeping cars in service nationwide.

The company also moved dramatically into the realm of railroad car building, including freight cars, as a result of merger with the nation's largest freight car builder, Haskell & Barker, in 1922. Pullman was reorganized in 1924 to separate the manufacturing division from The Pullman Company, and in 1927 another reorganization created Pullman Inc. to hold the capital stock of both the Pullman Company and the Pullman Car &

Manufacturing Company. In 1930 Pullman acquired another major car-building enterprise, the Standard Steel Car Company, resulting in another name change for the car-building arm, to Pullman-Standard.

The dramatic expansion of traffic during the 1920s forced the company to add about 300 to 400 cars annually to its roster. By the end of the decade in 1930, Pullman's fleet was at its largest with 9,801 cars staffed by 10,500 porters and maids. That same year, Pullman handled 29.3 million passengers, down from its all-time high of 39 million in the mid-1920s but still a staggering number when one considers that the figure represented over 80,000 passengers traveling daily on a Pullman car.

THE PULLMAN POOL AND SPECIAL EVENT SERVICES

In addition to a wide array of regularly scheduled services, Pullman operated vast numbers of special or seasonal movements. It seemed everybody had the disposable income to travel in style, consequently first-class travel for vacations and events grew enormously. One of the advantages to running a nationwide company was the ability to move staff and equipment to accommodate regionalized peak demands. For this eventuality, Pullman maintained a large pool of cars specifically for nomadic assignments. These cars could be shifted, for example, from northern operations to the South in winter, or from the East Coast to Western travel destinations, or to cool New England and Upper Michigan in summer. In between there was Mardi Gras in New Orleans in February, Easter vacation for families, and the Kentucky Derby in Louisville in May.

Pullman's Florida traffic in particular expanded dramatically, typically tripling in winter to require 900 cars each season in the mid-1920s. In the 1924–25 winter season,

text continued on page 52

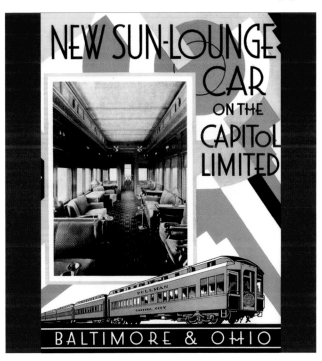

B&O produced this attractive brochure to advertise the new Pullman Sun-Lounge cars on its top train. The three cars—*Capitol Arms*, *Capitol City*, and *Capitol Square*—were built for the *Capitol Limited* in July 1929. Two other cars, *Capitol Courier* and *Capitol Escort*, were assigned to B&O's Washington–Detroit service. In this format, the open-platform end of an observation car was fully enclosed, sparing patrons the discomfort of smoke and road dust. Rolling stock of this type was sometimes also referred to as a "solarium" car. BALTIMORE & OHIO, JOE WELSH COLLECTION

In response to the Depression, railroads sought numerous ways to cut costs in the 1930s. Pullman helped by introducing restaurant-sleeping cars. Cars in this format offered a more cost effective option than maintaining a full dining car on trains with reduced patronage. Here, Chicago Great Western train No. 2, the *Minnesotan*, carries the Pullman restaurant-sleeper *Old Elm Club* on the rear at Forest Park, Illinois, in August 1934 as the train neared the end of its run at Chicago's Grand Central Station. The short train is typical of Depression-ravaged consists on secondary passenger carriers like Great Western, Katy, Soo Line, and Erie. A.W. JOHNSON, KRAMBLES-PETERSON ARCHIVE, JOE WELSH COLLECTION

The Pullman Conductor and Porter

The Pullman Company personnel aboard a train were under the supervision of the Pullman conductor, seen here on the far right with his staff on the platform of Chicago's Grand Central Station. Photographed in the 1920s, the crew stands ready to take Baltimore & Ohio's *Capitol Limited* to Washington, D.C. The train's barber is on the far left; next to him is a buffet attendant or bus boy. The six dapperly uniformed men to the right are porters for six sleeping cars.—*BALTIMORE & OHIO, WILLIAM F. HOWES JR. COLLECTION*

For 100 years, in the eyes of millions of travelers, the sleeping car-porter, attendant, and conductor embodied The Pullman Company. It was an image, nurtured by the company, that reached additional millions through portrayals of Pullman service in print, film, and even on the stage. The Pullman porter, in particular, entered American culture as an icon for courteous, attentive service offered with a smile, discretion, and civility. Because nearly all Pullman porters in America were African American, the position became part of a stereotype for the race, with implications both positive and negative. In time, Pullman porters would also come to represent the leading edge in a movement advancing economic freedom and civil rights for black Americans.

Car No. 9, one of two Chicago, Alton & St. Louis coaches remodeled into sleeping cars by George Pullman and his associate, Benjamin Field, made its inaugural run from Bloomington, Illinois, to Chicago on the night of September 1, 1859. In charge, as Pullman's "conductor" was 22-year old Jonathan L. Barnes. His responsibilities included familiarizing passengers with the new facilities, preparing berths, and maintaining discipline. (In that sense, he might also be considered as Pullman's first porter.) As Barnes recounted years later, "I remember on the first night I had to compel passengers to take their boots off before they got into the berths. They wanted to keep them on—seemed afraid to take them off." When it became apparent that it was going to take time to develop business for this new service, Pullman removed his conductors and relied on the railroad's trainmen to oversee the nightly conversion from coach to sleeping car and assist passengers.

Civilian sleeping-car service was curtailed during the Civil War so that the cars could be made available for military use. But once the conflict was over, public acceptance grew rapidly as major improvements were made in equipment design and service amenities. George Pullman led the way with his vision for a national network of sleeping-car lines offering comfortable accommodations, luxurious surroundings, and the amenities of a first-class hotel. This called for a consistently high level of personalized service. Pullman recognized that he needed personnel on the cars who would be under his management and whose sole duty would be to serve his customers.

Although sleeping-car operators had from time to time assigned porters to tend to the needs of passengers aboard their cars, it was not until about 1870 that George Pullman began employing black males exclusively for this purpose. Four million blacks had recently been emancipated from slavery. Many had worked in domestic service on the plantations of their owners. They had the experience and work ethic Pullman sought and they needed jobs. Also, the fact that Pullman's operations at the time were concentrated in the North attracted those who wanted to migrate away from the plantation environment. African American males would maintain their monopoly on Pullman porter positions for nearly a century, although jobs as attendants, bus boys, and cooks aboard Pullman's buffet and restaurant cars would be filled also by Filipino immigrants beginning in 1925.

Pullman's standards and expectations were high. The company came to favor young black men of about 25, with at least five years of work experience, in hopes that they were now ready to settle into a long career on the railroad. A new hire underwent rigorous training in the basic mechanical aspects of a Pullman car as well as service standards covering everything from berth preparation to the proper way to present and pour a beverage. Student trips under the tutelage of an experienced porter tested how well these lessons had been learned. A porter's performance would continue to be reviewed periodically throughout his career.

A sleeping-car porter tended to the needs of 15 to 20 passengers on a typical overnight trip. He saw his job as being a cross between a concierge, bellhop, valet, housekeeper, mechanic, baby sitter, and security guard. Formal responsibilities included setting up his car for service; greeting passengers, assisting them with their luggage to their accommodation, and explaining its features; preparing beds; providing or arranging for shoe shine, clothes pressing, and room services; maintaining a comfortable temperature in the car; making morning "wake-up" calls; and ensuring that each passenger detrained safely at his or her intended station. And, all the while, he was expected to be an "ambassador of good will" for the Pullman Company, prepared at any moment day or night to be a good listener, answer questions, find lost articles and handle emergencies.

Where two or more Pullman-operated cars were being handled in a train, a Pullman conductor was assigned to supervise all on-board Pullman personnel, collect and sell accommodation tickets, and perform-related record-keeping. These positions were nearly always filled by caucasian males. Unlike his railroad company counterpart whose responsibilities extended to the safe and efficient movement of the train over the road, the Pullman conductor focused solely on the accommodations and services being provided by the Pullman Company. When collecting and selling tickets on a train, the railroad's conductor picked up the portion covering transportation from origin to destination, while the Pullman conductor handled only the accommodation tickets and charges.

On trains made up largely or entirely of Pullman-operated cars, the Pullman conductor might oversee at least a dozen employees serving upward of 150 passengers occupying a hundred or more section and room accommodations. Where only one Pullman car was in service, the Pullman conductor's duties were handled by the car's porter functioning as a "porter in charge."

Most Pullman porters took pride in their work, embraced life out on the railroad, and passed their career down from generation to generation. But there was a downside to the job as well. The hours were long,

pay was modest, and having to rely on tips for a decent income could be downright demeaning. And then there was the issue of being addressed as "George," regardless of one's name. Perhaps it started because porters in George Pullman's employ were viewed by some people as simply an extension of antebellum tradition to modern industry. It had been common on plantations for slaves to

In a scene from a Pullman Company educational filmstrip, a business traveler is assisted by the Pullman conductor (left) and porter as he disembarks from brand-new sleeping cars built by Pullman-Standard for the Nickel Plate Road's new 1950 Chicago–Cleveland–Buffalo streamliner, the *Nickel Plate Limited.* WILLIAM F. HOWES JR. COLLECTION

take as their own a portion of their master's name. But whatever the reason, many porters found the practice objectionable. Some other people named George did as well. In fact, a passenger named George William Dulany, Jr., of Iowa, organized the "Society for the Prevention of Calling Sleeping Car Porters George." Soon the group was claiming membership in excess of 30,000, including such notable "Georges" as George Herman "Babe" Ruth and England's King George V.

Initially, all porters were paid the same wage without regard to the type of car they operated or their years of service. With expansion of the business, distinctions

were made between the various classes of Pullman service, wherein porters on the higher capacity parlor and tourist cars received more than those working in sleepers. Buffet and restaurant car attendants were the best paid. By 1920, pay was based upon length of service as well as class of service. Some of these and other improvements came from federal government control during World War I or through company endorsed employee organizations, such as the Employee Representation Plan. Still, low wages, long hours and other substandard working conditions prompted a group of porters to seek independent union representation. The Brotherhood of Sleeping Car Porters was formed in 1925, more than a decade after Pullman's conductors had successfully organized as the Order of Sleeping Car Conductors. The porters turned for leadership to A. Philip Randolph, a charismatic and controversial black social activist. Having no enthusiasm for unions, and particularly fearful of one headed by an avowed socialist, Pullman initially refused to recognize the Brotherhood. But in 1937, it finally negotiated its first contract with the porters' union. The Brotherhood soon became the most potent force within organized labor for black workers. It not only significantly improved the economic and working conditions of sleeping-car porters, but under Randolph's vision and leadership it was a driving force in the civil-rights movement. Despite these gains, porters were still effectively barred from positions traditionally held by caucasians, if not by company policy, by the lack of job opportunities as Pullman's business went into steep decline beginning in the late 1950s.

As more and more railroads took over their sleeping- and parlor-car operations from Pullman in the 1950s and 1960s, many Pullman porters and attendants simply transferred over to those roads until they could retire. For some, it even led to service with Amtrak after its formation in 1971. By contrast, most railroads did not need Pullman's conductors, leaving them to either retire or find employment elsewhere.

text continued from page 49

Florida-bound trains alone carried nearly a million passengers, most in Pullman cars and some from as far away as Quebec and Montana. Operating the pool required an encyclopedic memory of the vagaries of seasonal demand and an equal amount of creativity. Traffic to Florida required the use of large numbers of stateroom cars—many more than the average train usually carried. They had to be gathered judiciously, serviced, and properly positioned to handle the crowds when the railroads initiated the seasonal schedules of such trains as the *Florida Special* and the *Orange Blossom Special* each December.

The Florida and summer traffic was largely predictable, but uncommon demands were also handled with aplomb, thanks to Pullman's long experience with special moves. Serving conventions, presidential inaugurations,

and religious or business events was a regular way of life for Pullman which was then a principal means of travel between North American cities. Visiting dignitaries such as the Catholic Cardinals and their entourage of delegates enroute to Chicago for the 1926 Eucharistic Congress required the assembly of entire special trains, resulting in one of the largest single special moves in Pullman history—more cars than typically were reserved for the Florida traffic. The event occurred just once, but Pullman even managed to paint a group of cars used in the event in deep red (the color of vestments worn by a Cardinal) in honor of the men of God.

There were extra challenges, to be sure. Often, convention dates conflicted with one another and positioning the cars for special moves almost always required the relocation of empty equipment ("deadheading") over great distances to handle demand—an expensive undertaking. Sometimes the Pullman pool stood still, as it were, being used to provide supplementary hotel space. When convention room demand outstripped the ability of a local community to handle the rush, "Pullman Cities" were created. The Shriners' Convention of 1923 in Washington, D. C., for example, saw 473 Pullmans parked in ten different railroad yards, each a miniature city with temporary "streets" constructed between the tracks for passengers and Pullman employees, including company doctors and nurses, on hand to care for the guests.

In 1929, the Pullman Company had about 7,500 cars assigned to specific car lines between cities and 2,100 cars

in the Pullman pool; some cars traveled all over the country and beyond, while others remained in relatively stable orbit. Consider the nomadic life of the 6-compartment 3-drawing-room stateroom car *Glen Alta* assigned to the Pullman pool. The car celebrated New Years Day 1929 in chilly New York City, covered 149,784 miles in 365 days and ended the year in sunny Key West, Florida. In March alone, it called at Toronto, Miami, Los Angeles, and New

RIGHT: Pullman buffet and restaurant cars frequently supplemented railroad-operated food and beverage services and generally were available only to passengers occupying Pullman accommodations. Their use grew during the Great Depression of the 1930s when some railroads cut back on their dining-car operations. Here, a couple is being served in a heavyweight car of that era by a Pullman attendant. Notice Pullman's attractive "Indian Tree"-pattern china. THE NEWBERRY LIBRARY

FAR RIGHT: A Pullman lounge and club service menu from 1937 offered the standard Pullman fare including Martinis and Manhattans for 35 cents. JOE WELSH COLLECTION

BELOW: Not all sleeping cars in the heavyweight era were owned and operated by The Pullman Company. The Oostanaula was one of four cars built by Pullman in 1921 for the Central of Georgia. The standard 12-section 1-drawing-room car remained under CofG ownership and operation until it was sold to Pullman in 1925. although a steel car, the Oostanaula had a wood roof. It was reduced to tourist-car service in 1941, numbered 1171, and soon after was placed in troop-train service for the duration of World War II. The car was sold to the Chicago, Burlington & Quincy in 1947 and ended its days in maintenance-of-way service. SMITHSONIAN INSTITUTION, WILLIAM F. HOWES JR. COLLECTION

York, encountering temperatures ranging from 6 degrees to 86 degrees. The car was on the road 309 days of the year. By contrast, its fleet mate, the *Richard Henry Lee*, a parlor car in daytime service, spent the majority of the same year just traveling on a regular Pullman line between New York and Washington once a day.

SERVING SMALL-TOWN AMERICA —THE SETOUT SLEEPER

As a result of historians' overemphasis on Pullman's involvement in top "name" trains, Pullman is often perceived to have been primarily a purveyor of luxury accommodations for the rich. In fact, Pullman's main mission was to provide comfortable, reliable, safe travel to all comers—the company's slogan said as much. Nowhere

was this focus on the common man more obvious than in Pullman's willingness to offer sleeping-car service to the many smaller cities along its routes between major cities in the form of the "set-out" sleeper. Sleepers so designated were—often in the middle of the night—detached from the train, short of the train's terminating city, and "set out" at the car's destination station. If this happened at, say, 4 a.m., travelers could remain snug in their beds aboard the now-parked car until a saner hour, usually 7:30 or 8 a.m., when the car had to be vacated. The reverse arrangements allowed patrons to board the parked sleeper perhaps as early as 9 p.m. and turn in for the night. Later in the night, the sleeper would be picked up by a specific train passing through town and carried to the train's final destination. (Although the Pullman was not being set out

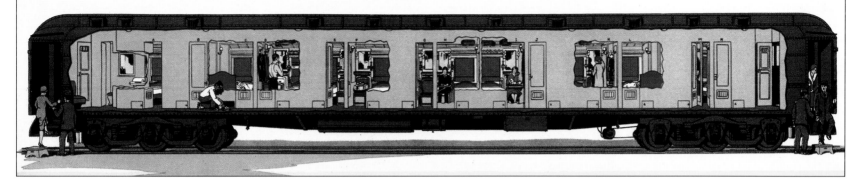

1927

THE SINGLE ROOM CAR The single room car, for over-night journeys, is a particular luxury to a large class of travelers. It contains 14 rooms, each for a single passenger, with full toilet facilities, stationary bed across the car, folding washstand with mirror and side lights above; drop shelf for writing or serving meals. Luggage space under bed, and in roomy racks. Cheval mirror inside door. Air intake in door, electric fan, thermos water bottle, individual heat control. The bed has box springs and spring mattress. Two or more rooms can be used *en suite* if desired.

in this instance, it was still referred to as a "set-out" sleeper, as that is how it arrived at the location.)

Despite it having been easier and more cost effective for the company simply to focus on the big cities and not switch sleepers in and out of a train during its run, Pullman provided hundreds of dedicated set-out sleeping-car lines nationwide to patrons in places like Elmira, New York; Oil City, Pennsylvania; Woodsville, New Hampshire; or Montgomery, Alabama. Set-out sleeper service reached its zenith in the 1920s. The cars were staffed by a smiling Pullman porter and featured the same crisp sheets and comfortable bed one could find on the top trains. It couldn't have been a sizable money maker for the company but the service was appreciated and relied on by thousands of people for decades.

DEPRESSION AND CRISIS

This orderly, conservative transportation world would come crashing down around Pullman, thanks to the massive stockmarket crash in the fall of 1929 and the onset of the Great Depression whose impact was more significant than anything Pullman had previously weathered. Those who still had jobs and still traveled, often went by the more economic coach class or used their own car to journey over a burgeoning network of new, government-sponsored roads. Pullman's sleeping-car traffic dropped by 58 percent from 1929 to 1933; its parlor-car market, more discretionary and more easily impacted by the rail coach trade, all but vaporized.

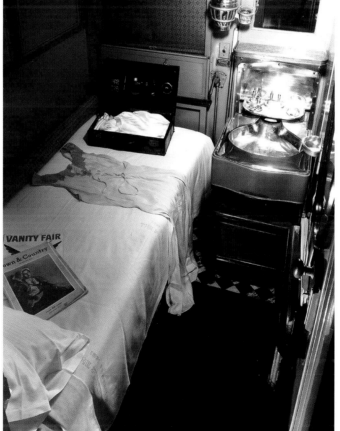

ABOVE: Pullman's response to its passengers' increasing desire for privacy was to create more cars with private rooms. In 1927, cars with 14 single bedrooms with stationary beds in the "Night" prefix series were introduced. This side view drawing from a Pullman brochure illustrates these single-bedroom cars. *THE PULLMAN COMPANY, JOE WELSH COLLECTION*

LEFT: This photo shows the interior of one of the new 1927 bedrooms with full toilet facilities and a folding wash stand with mirror. Above the open suitcase is the window shade and above the washstand is the trademark Pullman water bottle. *UNION PACIFIC RAILROAD MUSEUM, JOE WELSH COLLECTION*

The sleeping-car operation lost $1.2 million in 1932 and over $1.6 million in 1935. This was the first period during which the usually secure business lost money. Pullman took drastic steps to lure customers back to its cars. Upper-berth rates were cut first by 20 then 50 percent.

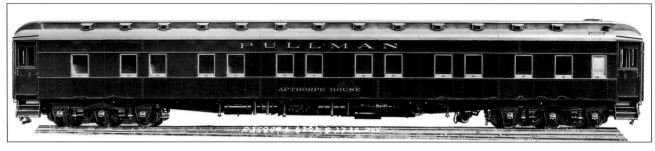

CHANGING TASTES AND NEW ACCOMMODATIONS

To attract riders, Pullman attempted to change the products it offered or to redefine them when it couldn't. In the early 1930s, the company began marketing the concept of the "single-occupancy section." For a marginally increased rate, the traveler could have an entire section to him- or herself, enjoying more privacy by not having to share accommodations with an upper berth mate. It was a smart attempt to glean more revenue from a bad situation. For some time, even before the onset of the Depression, Pullman had been struggling with the loss of upper-berth traffic. Ruminating on the merits of the open section in the 1930s, the Pennsylvania Railroad—a major Pullman customer—revealed, for example, that while it was able to fill 77 percent of its lower berths, it could only fill 18 percent of the uppers. Passengers now wanted more privacy than sections could offer. It was a particularly troublesome trend for Pullman, almost 50 percent of whose fleet comprised cars—the standard-bearer 12-1 and other cars heavy with sections—growing less desirable to its passengers every day.

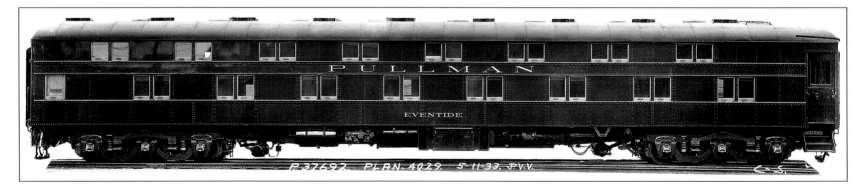

Following the 1931 introduction of the duplex single room design in cars *Wanderer* and *Voyager*, and under continuing pressure from the Pennsylvania Railroad to develop private-room cars with greater passenger capacity, in 1933 Pullman rebuilt two composite baggage-club cars into 16 duplex single-room sleepers named *Eventide* (shown here) and *Nocturne*. Previously, Pullman had been able to fit only 14 crosswise single bedrooms on one level in a car. Now, by staggering room levels in "split level" or "duplex" style, 16 rooms could be accommodated. Pullman eventually would standardize on a 12-duplex-single room 5-double-bedroom or, after World War II, a 12-duplex-single-room 4-double-bedroom configuration. *SMITHSONIAN INSTITUTION, WILLIAM F. HOWES JR. COLLECTION*

Pullman had also been working to provide the ideal single-occupancy room since 1927 when it introduced the "single bedroom" with a stationary bed, used only on brief overnight runs in a group of cars named in the *Night* series. This was followed by a bedroom with a bed convertible to a sofa and then to the double bedroom (1930) with a convertible sofa bed and an upper berth above it, used for two passengers. To squeeze more rooms into each car (thereby earning more revenue), Pullman first experimented with the "duplex" single-room car in 1931. The two rebuilt cars, named *Voyager* and *Wanderer*, contained single rooms on alternating levels; the rooms interlocked, with portions overlapping each other. The *Eventide* and *Nocturne*, experimental cars outfitted entirely with duplex-style rooms, followed in 1933. In 1931, too, Pullman introduced the private section and the enclosed section, each of which had curtains or a folding door for privacy, the former of which also had a tiny lavatory annex nearby.

In response to declining ridership and changing tastes, Pullman scrapped a significant number of its older, outdated cars and rebuilt many cars to contain more private rooms. It also rebuilt a number of cars to offer a mix of sleeping accommodations and dining or restaurant-lounge facilities. At first glance this would seem an odd trend for a company which had largely gotten out of the restaurant business by the 1920s, but shrinking patronage on Depression-era railroads coupled with the high operating expense of offering full dining cars had led to a trend where Pullman provided the railroad's meal service in its own cars using a floor space smaller than a full dining car and better tailored to the demand. For railroads with marginal dining-car traffic, using Pullman to provide some of the food-and-beverage service was a cost-effective option. Minor passenger carriers like the Erie Railroad and the Chicago Great Western relied heavily on Pullman's food service, and even the major carriers replaced full dining cars where they could.

AIR-CONDITIONING

By far, the greatest single improvement to the Pullman fleet in the 1930s, from a comfort standpoint, was the introduction of air-conditioning. Before air-conditioning became commonplace, Pullman had attempted to pre-cool its cars prior to boarding, but the effort was,

This full-page color ad touting the Single Occupancy Section appeared in *National Geographic* magazine in 1938. WILLIAM F. HOWES JR. COLLECTION

RIGHT: Erie Railroad's *Erie Limited* between Chicago and New York (Jersey City) was an example of a train that aspired to the greatness of its competitor, the *20th Century Limited.* Shown in the photo eastbound at Binghamton, New York, Pullman observation car *Monte Leone,* originally built for B&O's *Capitol Limited,* carries the train's marker lamps and drumhead in this view circa 1931. *CAL'S CLASSICS; BROCHURE, JOE WELSH COLLECTION*

BELOW: As the Depression deepened in 1932, Pullman restaurant service was offered on the *Erie Limited. Rio Sonora*—featuring 6 sections, a 32-seat dining room, and a mid-car kitchen—had been rebuilt in 1932 for service on the Southern Pacific Railroad of Mexico. It is shown at Hornell, New York. *CAL'S CLASSICS*

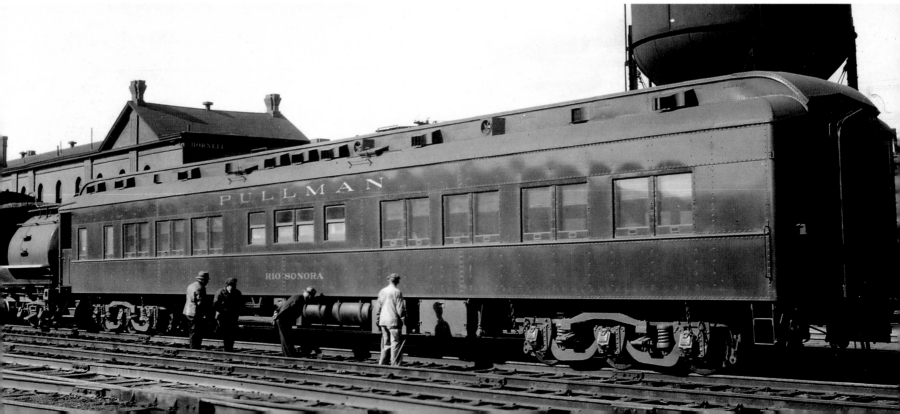

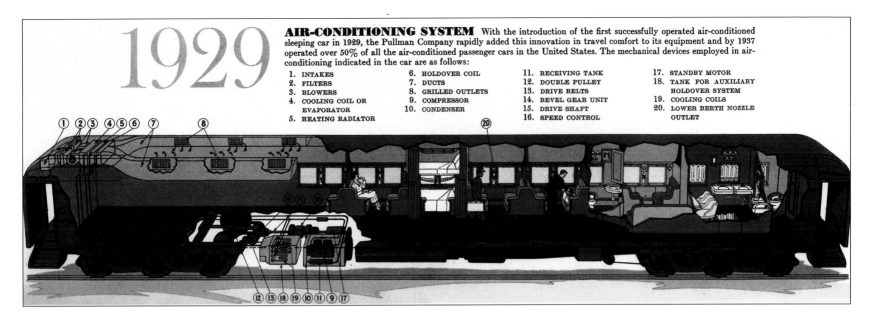

1929

AIR-CONDITIONING SYSTEM With the introduction of the first successfully operated air-conditioned sleeping car in 1929, the Pullman Company rapidly added this innovation in travel comfort to its equipment and by 1937 operated over 50% of all the air-conditioned passenger cars in the United States. The mechanical devices employed in air-conditioning indicated in the car are as follows:

1. INTAKES
2. FILTERS
3. BLOWERS
4. COOLING COIL OR EVAPORATOR
5. HEATING RADIATOR
6. HOLDOVER COIL
7. DUCTS
8. GRILLED OUTLETS
9. COMPRESSOR
10. CONDENSER
11. RECEIVING TANK
12. DOUBLE PULLEY
13. DRIVE BELTS
14. BEVEL GEAR UNIT
15. DRIVE SHAFT
16. SPEED CONTROL
17. STANDBY MOTOR
18. TANK FOR AUXILIARY HOLDOVER SYSTEM
19. COOLING COILS
20. LOWER BERTH NOZZLE OUTLET

at best, marginally successful, especially when a car had been sitting in the sun in a stifling hot coach yard all day. Once the cars were on the move, screened windows let in fresh air, but they failed to keep out the grime that was indigenous to steam-era railroading. After a run, veteran porters could tell where a car had been simply by the color of the thin layer of dust covering everything inside: red for the Deep South, gray for the Western plains, and so forth. Air-conditioning changed all that, transforming the cars into a comfortable sleeping environment and eliminating the dust problem. It was also a novelty. Virtually, no American home featured air-conditioning in the 1930s, and sometimes people rode the train just to escape the heat.

Pullman had experimented with electro-mechanical air-conditioning in 1927 with the sleeper *Jacksonville*, but it was a failure. In 1929, sleeper *McNair* received an ice-based system in which circulating air was passed over blocks of ice carried under the car. Technology evolved over the next few years to make the ice-based air-conditioning more reliable (such systems lasted on some North American passenger trains well into the 1970s). In 1930, the B&O held successful tests, and in 1931 it introduced what it advertised as the first completely air-conditioned train in America, the *Columbian*. By the next year, B&O had re-equipped much of its fleet with air-conditioning. A number of other railroads followed suit to the point where by 1935, ten percent of the cars in service nationwide were air-conditioned.

Pullman grasped the significance of air-conditioning immediately. Air-conditioning its existing cars would make the fleet more attractive while helping employ hundreds of its shopworkers idled by the Depression. By 1936, Pullman had over 2,300 air-conditioned cars in operation. One year later it added a thousand more and by the beginning of World War II it would complete its air-conditioning program having re equipped all but its oldest cars.

STREAMLINING

More than just minor changes in accommodations or air-conditioning would be required to blunt the massive drop in ridership caused by the Depression. By the early 1930s, the railroad industry would turn its attention to changing the very shape of its passenger trains as a way to attract the public's attention—and dollars. Streamlining, creating sleek new trains and railroad cars, would turn out to be the single most important change in American passenger railroading.

Along the way, as the streamlining revolution unfolded in the mid-to-late 1930s, brand-new types of streamlined Pullman cars would be developed individually or as part of whole new trains. Pullman's manufacturing and operating arms would take a leading role in the effort, creating and staffing many of the fabulous new cars and trains. But Pullman had a dark side too. Its overly aggressive efforts to protect its turf, as other carbuilders challenged its supremacy, would sow the seeds of a major anti-trust suit that would change Pullman forever.

In 1929, air-conditioning caption was a rare treat to be encountered. Virtually no homes had air-conditioning at the time. Pullman pioneered the concept, which it explained in this cutaway advertisement. JOE WELSH COLLECTION

3

The Pullman Company
introduces the
"ROOMETTE"

Desperate to regain passenger traffic lost during
the Depression, American railroads and Pullman tried everything.
They cut fares, rebuilt older cars to offer more appealing accommodations, and added air-conditioning to their fleets. It wasn't enough.
What was needed was an improvement so dramatic that it galvanized
public attention. It came in the form of the railroad streamliner
beginning in the early 1930s. Comprising exciting, futuristic shapes
and colors, pulled by new motive power (diesel-electrics, usually) and
made of new lightweight metals such as aluminum, the streamliner
would turn out to be the single most significant improvement ever
made in American passenger railroading.

The Pullman Company had suffered from an image of being
outdated and conservative for years. Secure in its earnings as a
monopoly, for decades it had spent virtually nothing on advertising
to update that image. Its fleet of older, dark green heavyweight cars
did little to bolster the company's appeal. Now as a result of the
Depression, Pullman was suddenly afflicted with a significant
decline in revenues; its sleeping-car business lost $3.3 million
between 1932 and 1935. Given the circumstances, one would have

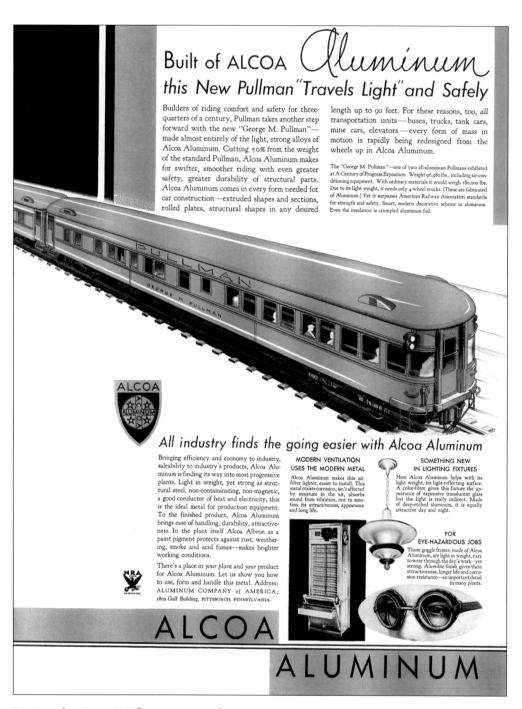
thought that Pullman would embrace streamlining with open arms. Instead it took an ambiguous approach.

Ironically, as both a manufacturer and an operator of cars on the railroads, Pullman Incorporated's manufacturing interests didn't necessarily match its operating interests. The conservative Pullman (operating) Company was disposed to rely on the large, remodeled fleet of heavyweight cars in which it was investing heavily. To attract customers, by 1935 Pullman would spend about $24.5 million to upgrade that fleet with air-conditioning. Due to this costly effort and the uncertainty caused by Depression, The Pullman Company was reluctant to jump into the wholesale creation of an expensive new fleet of streamlined sleeping cars which would render its existing heavyweight cars obsolete overnight.

But Pullman Car & Manufacturing was an entirely different story; it had to live in the feast-or-famine world of railroad car-building. In 1930 the company had earned $10 million; over the next three years, the heart of the Great Depression, it lost it all. Worse, it appeared for a time that the market for new cars had all but vanished. PC&M was a giant builder theoretically capable of producing as many as 113,000 freight cars and 3,000 passenger cars per year. But in 1932, the depths of the Depression, Pullman's vast manufacturing business came to a virtual standstill. That year it made only 252 freight cars, two trolley cars, and four railroad passenger cars.

PC&M desperately needed to maintain its position as a leader in the industry. If the future demanded lightweight streamliners, Pullman would build the future. But The Pullman (operating) Company would proceed more cautiously for a couple of reasons—the Depression's economic uncertainty might leave it with a whole fleet of new cars it couldn't use. And the schizophrenic nature of the railroad industry regarding streamliners didn't help. Some railroads readily embraced lightweight construction,

Experimental car *George M. Pullman* was constructed primarily of aluminum. It served as a bridge between the heavyweight car era and the lightweight era. Completed in May 1933 it contained 1 drawing room, 3 double bedrooms, 1 compartment, a buffet, and an observation lounge. It served on trains such as the *Chief* before it was withdrawn from Pullman service and sold to the Chicago Great Western in 1952. The photo at right shows its as-built appearance. *AD, ALCOA, JOE WELSH COLLECTION; PHOTO, ARTHUR D. DUBIN COLLECTION*

PULLMAN IN THE EARLY STREAMLINED ERA

Major structural progress in Pullman car development had been slow since the switch to all-steel construction in 1910. In addition to air-conditioning, a major improvement, the list of technical "advancements" was limited largely to interior space changes. In an effort to meet public demand, Pullman had reworked its interior designs to come up with more enclosed accommodations such as the single bedroom (1927), the double bedroom (1930), and the duplex single room (1931). Pullman

while others, uncertain about the safety or utility of the concept, avoided it.

once boasted about the solid comfort of its heavy sleepers, stating that just the trucks on a modern heavyweight Pullman car outweighed the entire wooden cars it used to build. Now that solid, ponderous bulk had become a marketing liability. Americans wanted to be associated with sleek new things, fast things.

In response, in 1932 PC&M began work on a radical new car built almost entirely of aluminum. The result was the *George M. Pullman*. Instead of solemn dark green, the new car was built of shiny aluminum. At 48 tons, it weighed a little more than half what a standard Pullman car weighed. Even its trucks and wheels were principally crafted of aluminum. The car also featured the first

A rare color view of the *George M. Pullman* shows the car sitting at the Chicago Great Western facilities in Oelwein, Iowa, on June 12, 1950. Two years later, CGW purchased the car. Note that it now rides on six-wheel trucks and sports a Pullman "pool" livery of solid gray accented by white stripes.—*HARRY STEGMAIER COLLECTION*

enclosed, rounded solarium on its end. Much refined, this tear-drop-shaped enclosure would become a hallmark of many future observation cars. The *George M. Pullman* was displayed at the Century of Progress Exhibition in 1933—the pride and joy of both Pullman and Alcoa Aluminum.

The *George M. Pullman* was long-lived, being retired from Pullman service in 1952 and surviving on the Chicago Great Western Railway until it was scrapped in 1964. But it was a one-of-a-kind, transitional car. Pullman's next adventure in streamlining would revolutionize the industry. The progressive Union Pacific Railroad, concerned about the impacts of the Depression and intent on gaining back the traffic it had lost, contracted with PC&M to create a true streamliner in 1933. The goal was to build an economical—read, lightweight—train. Pullman created a three-car (including the power car), low-slung, 204-foot-long articulated (jointed) train that weighed about 85 tons—less than one heavyweight dining car. Constructed by Pullman primarily of aluminum and equipped with a distillate-engine Winton power plant from Electro Motive Corporation (a subsidiary of General Motors), the canary yellow speedster—identified as the M-10000—was unveiled in February 1934. It went on a nationwide tour—even being inspected by President Franklin D. Roosevelt—before being displayed at the Century of Progress Exhibition in Chicago between May and July 1934. Millions would see the sleek new train in person or hear about its exploits on the radio.

THE TRAIN THAT HAS WRITTEN THE MOST COLORFUL PAGE IN TRANSPORTATION HISTORY

SPEED with comfort, safety and economy of operating costs were the aims in the construction of Union Pacific's new train. Because of its radical departure from the conventional type of car and train construction, exhaustive tests were conducted during the development of every feature of the train to insure its perfection. The train is built entirely of aluminum alloys, one-third the weight of steel with the same strength. ● Its 600 horse-power, distillate-burning, 12 cylinder, V-type motor, directly connected to a generator provides the power to drive two 300 horsepower electric motors which propel the train. A dual system of super brakes and a number of other especially designed appliances insure perfect safety. ● Articulated construction—the cars hinged together with only one truck between each two cars—provides smoother riding at high speeds. Roller bearings and especially designed trucks improve riding comfort and eliminate noise. The train is fully air-conditioned—no dust, no dirt, no drafts, and maintains a comfortable, uniform temperature during the heat of summer and chill of winter. An indirect lighting system sheds a uniform light, without shadows or glare. The newly designed

seats for 116 passengers in the two coaches assure utmost comfort. Individual trays are provided for each seat for meal service or writing purposes. Meals are prepared in the unique buffet-kitchen built into the rear of last car. ● The new type Pullman sleeping car is even more radically different in construction. Every berth, both upper and lower, has an individual washbowl and mirrored cabinet. Many new comforts and conveniences have been provided. Each seat has an adjustable arm rest. Windows are larger and provide an unobstructed view. Upper and lower berths in sections 1 and 2 are 6 feet, 9 inches long (6 inches longer than present berths) and were designed especially for tall persons. Aluminum louvre construction has supplemented the present-day curtains for sleeping car sections, and insures perfect ventilation in these air-conditioned cars. ● This train is not an experiment. During the early spring of 1934 it made a 12,625-mile test and exhibition trip from the Atlantic to the Pacific coast. (The Pullman car was not a part of the original three-car train which made this epochal trip.) It was exhibited in 68 cities in which 1,195,609 persons passed through to inspect its every feature. In addition hundreds of thou-

sands saw the exterior of the train only. Number 1 visitor was President Franklin D. Roosevelt. In the course of this historic trip, practically every kind of climatic condition was encountered. Temperatures varied from 10 degrees below zero to 92 degrees above. Snow, high winds, rain and dust storms provided unusual tests for the air-conditioning equipment. The train negotiated every sort of grade and curve from sea-level to altitudes of over 8000 feet. In special tests immediately following the epochal tour, a speed of 111 miles per hour was attained in the face of a 32-mile per hour head wind. At all times, under all circumstances, the super brakes and numerous other safety devices, in fact all the mechanical features functioned perfectly. ● This train is the first step in a pioneering program of rail transportation development. Union Pacific will soon place in service a 6-car train, including 3 Pullmans, between Chicago and the Pacific Coast. Two 9-car trains of similar design are also under construction and will be placed in transcontinental service immediately upon delivery. In its new, constructive program, Union Pacific is upholding a tradition as old as itself—**first with the finest in transportation facilities.**

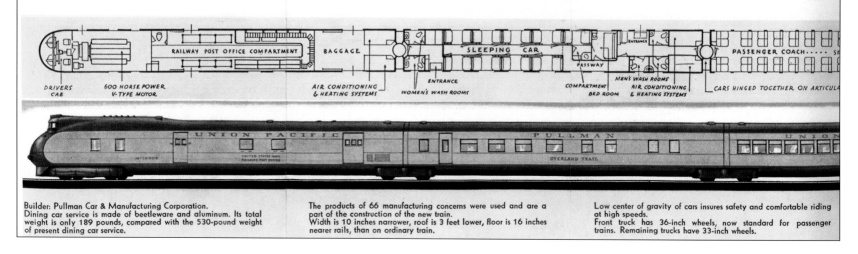

RAILWAY POST OFFICE COMPARTMENT BAGGAGE SLEEPING CAR ENTRANCE PASSENGER COACH····· SE

DRIVERS CAB 600 HORSE POWER V-TYPE MOTOR AIR CONDITIONING & HEATING SYSTEMS ENTRANCE WOMEN'S WASH ROOMS PASSWAY COMPARTMENT BED ROOM MEN'S WASH ROOMS AIR CONDITIONING & HEATING SYSTEMS CARS HINGED TOGETHER ON ARTICULA

UNION PACIFIC M-10000 UNITED STATES MAIL RAILWAY POST OFFICE PULLMAN OVERLAND TRAIL UNION

Builder: Pullman Car & Manufacturing Corporation.
Dining car service is made of beetleware and aluminum. Its total weight is only 189 pounds, compared with the 530-pound weight of present dining car service.

The products of 66 manufacturing concerns were used and are a part of the construction of the new train.
Width is 10 inches narrower, roof is 3 feet lower, floor is 16 inches nearer rails, than on ordinary train.

Low center of gravity of cars insures safety and comfortable riding at high speeds.
Front truck has 36-inch wheels, now standard for passenger trains. Remaining trucks have 33-inch wheels.

In time for the fair, in February 1934 Pullman produced a streamlined sleeper for the M-10000 named the *Overland Trail*. The *Overland Trail* featured 8 enclosed sections, 1 compartment, and 1 double bedroom. The car would never actually operate in the M-10000. It was withdrawn from the little speedster before it entered revenue service as a coach train linking Kansas City, Topeka, and Salina, Kansas. Initially as the *The Streamliner* and later as the *City of Salina*, the M-10000 would run from January 31, 1935, to December 16, 1941, before being removed from service and scrapped as a source of aluminum for the war effort.

Instead, the *Overland Trail* became part of UP's next new streamliner trainset—also a PC&M/EMC product—

LEFT: The *City of Portland,* inaugurated in June 1935 between Chicago and Portland, Oregon, via the C&NW and the UP carried the first regularly assigned lightweight, articulated Pullman sleepers. Car *Abraham Lincoln* offered 10 enclosed sections, 1 compartment, and 1 double bedroom while Overland Trail and Oregon Trail included 8 sections, 1 compartment, and 1 bedroom. The inaugural brochure (INSET) featured photos and floor plans of all car types on the new *City of Portland.* The train is pictured here operating on the C&NW at Maywood, Illinois, on July 18, 1935. Note the crowd gathered to watch its passing. Streamliners were still a novelty in the 1930s. *PHOTO: A. W. JOHNSON, KRAMBLES-PETERSON ARCHIVE; BROCHURE: UP, JOE WELSH COLLECTION*

65

Spacious, beautiful lounge and observation rooms make Pullman travel a pleasure.

THE
PULLMAN
COMPANY

presents a

Travel Innovation

THE "TWO-CAR UNIT"

adequate for those desiring to read at night. The windows of the observation room have fabric window shades of blue with horizontal silver stripes. In the lounge are venetian blinds of satin aluminum finish. Some of the bedrooms in both cars have the blue color scheme noted in the observation-lounge, the upholstery being a rose color and the carpets of a rust tint. In other rooms the upholstery is in green, with the decorating in graduating shades of tan.

The two-car unit was designed and produced by Pullman-Standard Car Manufacturing Company for the Pullman Company, and will be experimentally operated in various sections of the country to demonstrate the value of such units as a nucleus for streamlined trains.

THE TWO-CAR UNIT

PULLMAN'S latest production for improved travel facilities is a lightweight streamlined articulated two-car unit so constructed that it can be used in a train with regular standard type cars. Starting with a unit of this kind as a foundation, an entire lightweight train can be gradually built up, by adding single or articulated units of similar design, until the desired consist of train is reached.

The two cars with alloy steel in the body construction, and predominantly aluminum alloy in the interior finish, weigh about the same as one standard steel car.

The first car of the unit named "Advance" is of the type known as "duplex" and contains 16 rooms. There are two regular bedrooms with upper and lower berth accommodations and 14 single rooms equally divided between rooms on the floor level and others reached by three steps. This duplex arrangement is the result of experiments during the last four years. In January, 1932, two sleeping cars, the "Voyager" and the "Wanderer," containing 10 standard sections and four "duplex" rooms, two upstairs and two down, began operation out of New York City and are in regular service today. In May, 1933, the second "duplex" experiment, consisting of two cars, "Eventide" and "Nocturne," with compartment type rooms on two levels, were placed in service and are still operated.

The exterior finish of the unit is of gunmetal shade, set off by black and gold striping, above and below the windows. The exterior contour has a skirt below the underframe covering the air-conditioning equipment, lighting batteries, water tanks, etc., visible on the ordinary car.

In the "Advance" a return is made to the transverse bedroom type of accommodation, with a daytime sofa that is convertible into a bed. There

are individual toilet facilities, with lighting, heating and cooling regulated in each room, the latter made possible by Pullman mechanical air-conditioning system for the whole car. The upper berth has a locker above the sofa for luggage. In the lower room luggage space is under the sofa and an overnight rack. The lower rooms are equipped with small lockers, from which the porter can take and replace the shoes of sleeping passengers, the upper occupants placing theirs on the stairway.

The rooms have many attractive facilities. There is an aluminum table that folds against the wall, which may be used for writing, serving of meals and other purposes. Arm rests folding into the back of the sofa form a comfortable feature. In the double bedrooms there is a fabric holder with compartments for small sundry articles. Six of the downstairs "duplex" rooms are en suite and a sliding partition can transform them into three large rooms. Four of the upper rooms have communicating doors.

The second car of the unit, named "Progress" contains a compartment and three double bedrooms, two of which are en suite. At the head of the observation-lounge is a buffet containing a broiler, coffee urn, and ice-cooled refrigerators. Monel metal is used in the broiler. The observation-lounge occupies practically half the length of the car. The furniture is of modern design, with tubular aluminum frames, and the upholstery is in the newest shades of blue, terra cotta, brown and rose.

There are two sections to the spacious observation end of the car. At the rounded end is an observation parlor seating six, while the lounge seats 20 and has sofas and section seats with tables. The ceiling is in light ivory, the walls a soft gray-blue and the base a darker shade of the same. Around the walls runs a panel in opalescent brown lacquer, above which is concealed a trough containing the electric light. The lighting feature is indirect and is

Although lower level rooms are for single occupancy, there is ample room for daylight visits.

View of upper room showing short stairway from the car floor level.

Occupants of upper rooms have lockers for storing luggage.

Ample space, comfortable sofa by day that becomes a spring bed at night, individual toilet facilities and regulation of light, heat and temperature.

the M-10001. Like its tiny predecessor, this train traveled the country on an exhibition tour before entering revenue service in June 1935 between Chicago and Portland as the *City of Portland*. This train actually contained three streamlined sleeping cars. In addition to the *Overland Trail*, the train offered the *Abraham Lincoln* with 10 enclosed sections, 2 compartment and 1 double bedroom and the *Oregon Trail* with a similar floor plan to the

round-end solarium observation car—with the *Advance*, containing 14 duplex single rooms and 2 double bedrooms. Unlike the early UP cars, which were undersized and constructed of aluminum, this pair was closer to a standard-size set of cars and constructed of Cor-Ten steel. Hardly had the paint dried on these unconventional lightweights when Pullman introduced the *Forward* in late 1936. Full-sized, non-articulated, first to incorporate a truss-side frame, sheathed in fluted stainless steel and containing 8 sections, 2 compartments and 2 double bedrooms, the *Forward* was the suitable prototype for a future fleet of conventional streamlined Pullman cars. But as an operator, Pullman, for the reasons outlined above, refused to commit to a wholesale re-equipping of its mammoth fleet. Instead it continued to rely on its existing heavyweight cars. It was the railroads, not Pullman, that truly led the early drive to streamline. And some carriers showed no predisposition to wait for Pullman to re-equip. If Pullman's ponderous operating arm wasn't going to take the lead in introducing lightweight sleepers on their road, the railroads would look elsewhere.

BUSINESS COMPETITION AND CONFLICT

Pullman's car-building competitors took advantage of the railroads' interest in streamlining. In 1935, builder American Car & Foundry constructed an attractive articulated streamliner for an unlikely buyer, the Gulf Mobile & Northern, which operated it between the endpoints of Jackson, Tennessee, and New Orleans. The little train included a sleeper-observation car with 6 sections and a drawing room. This sleeper was staffed by GM&N, not Pullman, employees.

BROCHURE, FACING PAGE: *Advance* and *Progress* were constructed of Cor-Ten steel in August 1936. Articulated (sharing a truck) to save weight, they operated together as a pair. *Advance* had 14 duplex single rooms and 2 double bedrooms; *Progress* offered 4 double bedrooms, a buffet, and an observation-lounge. First introduced in experimental service, they were renamed *Bear Flag* and *California Republic* respectively in 1937 and operated on the famous *Forty Niner*.
PULLMAN COMPANY, JOE WELSH COLLECTION

LEFT: The observation-lounge of *Progress* was an Art Deco masterpiece.
PULLMAN COMPANY, TRANSPORT HISTORY PRESS, JOE WELSH COLLECTION

Overland Trail. Union Pacific would introduce numerous new articulated streamliners over the next few years linking Chicago and Denver, San Francisco, and Los Angeles, all built by Pullman.

But interestingly, except for the UP trains, no other lightweight Pullmans were developed until 1936 when Pullman produced the novel two-car articulated set, the *Advance* and the *Progress*, which combined the *Progress*—a

Text continued on page 70

What's in a Car Name?

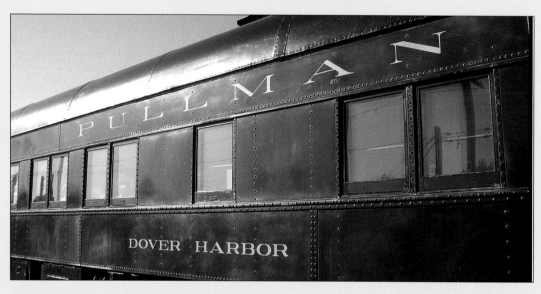

ABOVE: Wearing its name and heritage proudly in gold on Pullman green, restaurant-lounge *Dover Harbor* gleams in the sunlight. Names rather than numbers identified the majority of Pullman's cars, setting them apart from a railroad's fleet and evoking images of far-off places served by the Pullmans of yesteryear. *KARL ZIMMERMANN*

Y ou first glimpsed it through a lazy wisp of steam as you walked along the platform to your sleeping or parlor car. Materializing out of the gloom, each Pullman bore on its shiny flanks a unique name below its windows. Lending personality to an otherwise undistinguished rail carriage, names like *Cascade Echo* or *David Crockett* evoked far-off places or famous historical figures. Sometimes a car's name made immediate sense to the casual observer. Pullman's *Delaware Rapids*, for example, could frequently be found crossing its namesake river at Trenton, New Jersey, on the Pennsylvania Railroad. But how did a car with the unpronounceable

southwest Indian name of *Tchirege* sometimes end up in New York City's Penn Station?

Although the names of Pullman cars might not have always made sense to the uninitiated, the concept dated to the beginnings of the Pullman Company and existed as a way to keep track of Pullman's far-flung fleet. The decision to name rather than number most Pullman cars had its roots in both tradition and common sense. At the time of Pullman's creation in 1867, it was still common for American railroads to name both railroad cars and locomotives. And, as the industry evolved to a point where most railroad-owned cars and locomotives were numbered, Pullman continued to name its own cars to avoid confusion with the railroads on whose trains it operated. Some of Pullman's very earliest cars were lettered "A", "B" etc., but since there were only 26 letters to choose from in the alphabet, car names became the norm for the remainder of the company's history. Typically, the names were chosen by Pullman's Superintendent of Transportation or his staff, with the railroads also providing advice on the naming of cars for particularly important trains.

Even in its earliest days Pullman nomenclature relied heavily (but not completely) on geography for inspiration. As the fleet grew and Pullman scrambled to find appropriate names for new cars, virtually every major town or recognizable place in America would eventually come to be immortalized on the side of a Pullman. There was even a Pullman baggage-buffet-club car named *Wissinoming*, a small neighborhood in northeast Philadelphia where the author was raised.

Sometimes there was predictability to the pattern of names. Parlor cars, for example, were often named after women or flowers. But just as often, in the early decades of the company, there seemed to be no rhyme or reason to the choice of appellation. Pity the yardmaster or clerk having to deal with the names of hundreds of 12-section 1-drawing-room cars like *Abyssinia*, *Ontelaunee*, *Sapulpa*, or *Zephon*.

BELOW: There was a pattern to Pullman car names. Poplar-prefix names were applied to cars that contained six sections and six double bedrooms. *Poplar Shore*, formerly the *Taurus*, is shown in 1965. *HARRY STEGMAIER*

Mercifully, as Pullman's fleet grew to massive proportions in the early 1920s, car names were deliberately applied in series to allow employees to more easily identify a car's floor plan. Often a common prefix or suffix was used to identify a car's type. The first known example of this practice occurred in 1899 with a fleet of observation cars named in the *Ben* series: *Ben Avon*, *Ben Lomond*, etc. But it would be 21 years later as Pullman's fleet grew to 7,726 cars that the practice returned in earnest. In 1920, 50 new cars in the *Fort*-prefix series arrived with 10 sections, 1 drawing room, and 2 compartments. They were followed by similar cars in the *Camp* and *Cape* prefix series and shortly after by 24 cars with 12 sections and 1 drawing room named in the *St.* series such as *St. Lawrence*. Next, in 1924 and 1925 came a truly massive series of 335 cars in the *Mc* prefix series (*McAdam* to *McZena*) with 12 sections and 1 drawing room. Sometimes the names also hinted at assignment to a specific railroad or train. For example, cars with 8 sections, 1 drawing room, and 2 compartments built for service on the Chicago, Rock Island & Pacific were conveniently named in the *Rock* prefix series.

By the mid- to late 1920s, the majority of new Pullman cars being delivered were named in recognizable series. Eventually yardmasters assembling a train no longer were required to possess an encyclopedic memory of thousands of cars with one-of-a-kind names. Exceptions still abounded, though. Heavyweight tourist sleepers were typically numbered, not named. Rather than having cars named in logical series, some trains received cars with the names of important historical personalities in the territory they served. Great Northern's famous heavyweight train of 1929, the *Empire Builder*, had "sun parlor" observation cars named after men prominent in the early history of the GN such as James J. Hill, the road's founder whose nickname was applied to the

Parked at Louisville Union Station in 1969, L&N 6-section 6-roomette 4-double-bedroom *Louisiana Pine* is an example of a car bearing a geography-themed name.—*TOM SMART, HARRY STEGMAIER COLLECTION*

train. Sleeping cars were named for pioneers and soldiers who built the Northwest such as Henry H. Sibley, a fur trader and Indian fighter, or Charles A. Broadwater, a wagonmaster, trader, banker, and founder of the Montana Central Railway, a line eventually absorbed into the GN. Likewise, Southern Railway's *Crescent Limited* operating between New York and New Orleans had a similar rake of cars named for famous Southerners.

There were also intangible advantages to naming cars after on-line geographical points. Into the streamlined era, the use of the names of on-line cities, counties, or landmarks provided a marketing opportunity for the road to which the car normally was assigned. Sometimes the concept backfired. A competing railroad may have already chosen the name, for example. In one hilarious exchange, the Pennsylvania Railroad proudly notified an important shipper, Timken Roller Bearing, that it would shortly begin operating a new lightweight Pullman car named after Timken's home town, the City of Canton, Ohio. Timken shot back a note to the Pennsy informing the railroad that it didn't much care, for it had learned that the car *City of Canton* was riding on the roller bearings of Timken's bitter rival SKF!

And occasionally it seemed the practice of naming cars in easily understood series was regressing. Southern Pacific and Northern Pacific went so far as to remove previously applied names in favor of numbers on their assigned lightweight Pullmans. Lightweight sleepers built for assignment to the Santa Fe in 1938 had amazingly tongue-twisting Indian names like *Tyuonyi* and *Nankoweap*. So did sleepers

built after World War II for the Delaware, Lackawanna & Western. It was all part of the fascinating lore of Pullman car nomenclature. From the beginning to the end of Pullman service, the practice of naming rather than just numbering sleeping and parlor cars remained the norm rather than the exception. And the concept survives today. Amtrak's modern Superliner II and Viewliner sleepers still carry names on their flanks with regular Superliner II sleepers named for states, a practice in effect in 1867 when Pullman was established. It seems history and good ideas have a way of repeating themselves.

Some famous car series and their accommodations:

Heavyweight era (new construction):
Fort prefix (10 sections, 1 drawing room, 2 compartments)
Mc prefix (12 sections, 1 drawing room)
Glen prefix (6 compartments, 3 drawing rooms)
Night prefix (14 single bedrooms)
House suffix (13 double bedrooms)
Lake prefix (10 sections, 1 drawing room, 2 compartments)

Heavyweight era (rebuilt):
Clover prefix (8 sections, 5 double bedrooms)
Poplar prefix (6 sections, 6 double bdrms.)

Lightweight era:
American prefix (6 sections, 6 roomettes, 4 double bedrooms)
Cascade prefix (10 roomettes, 5 double bedrooms)
City prefix (17 roomettes, 1 section or 18 roomettes)
County suffix (13 double bedrooms)
Imperial prefix (4 double bedrooms, 4 compartments, 2 drawing rooms)
River suffix (10 roomettes, 6 double bedrooms)
Pacific prefix (10 roomettes, 6 double bedrooms)
Inn suffix (21 roomettes)

The Truss-type sleeping car offers every modern convenience

The interior color scheme of the main body of the car is in three shades of tan. The sections are upholstered in mauve color mohair. The carpet throughout the main body of the car is in green rust and plaid design. The bedrooms are in the same combination of tan colors, and the two compartments are finished in three shades of blue. The overhead lighting is semi-indirect and the lower berth lighting fixtures are of spherical design with blue night lights.

"FORWARD"

with PULLMAN's latest light weight unit

THE ALLOY STEEL TRUSS-FRAME

SLEEPING CAR

Every comfort for complete travel relaxation

Pullman courtesy makes traveling a pleasure

Semi-privacy for individual accommodations

The Double Bedrooms offer every traveling convenience

THE latest product of The Pullman Company is a sleeping car of steel alloy and truss-frame construction. This car, named FORWARD is over 40 per cent lighter in weight than a standard Pullman car of the same type of accommodations, which in this case consist of eight sections, two double bedrooms and two compartments. In building the FORWARD Pullman designers have attained the ultimate in light weight high tensile steel construction with the use of a truss-type of side frame to carry the entire load. The principle is that of the steel skyscraper, the strength of which lies in the frame. In this new car-body the frame is entirely welded, which eliminates the necessity of overlapping any of the framing parts, which would mean additional weight. Every part of the FORWARD construction has been carefully checked and tested until 220 per cent of the calculated maximum safe load had been applied. The car has rolling steps, not visible when the train is in motion, and another important feature is the tight-lock couplers with rubber draft gears, that absorb the shocks of starting and stopping. There are upper berth windows, as in all the latest Pullman sleepers.

Forward was the prototype for a future fleet of streamlined Pullmans. Full sized, non-articulated, constructed of stainless steel and the first lightweight sleeper with a truss side frame, the car inspired future cars for the Santa Fe and Rock Island. PULLMAN COMPANY, JOE WELSH COLLECTION

Forward is shown at La Junta, Colorado, in January 1937 in the consist of Santa Fe train 17, the westbound *Super Chief*. The car contained 8 sections, 2 compartments and 2 double bedrooms. The car is painted gray with a black roof and black-and-gold stripes above and below the windows, a change from the unpainted stainless steel it wore when it was advertised in Pullman's brochure. OTTO PERRY, DENVER PUBLIC LIBRARY, WESTERN HISTORY COLLECTION, IMAGE NO. OP-14528

Text continued from page 67

A much more serious threat came from a Philadelphia concern, the Edward G. Budd Manufacturing Company. In 1934 it had constructed the country's first diesel-powered, articulated streamliner, *Zephyr* 9900, for the Chicago, Burlington & Quincy Railroad. Additional Burlington *Zephyrs*, notably the *Twin Zephyrs* between Chicago and Minneapolis/St. Paul, Minnesota, and the *Mark Twain Zephyr* between Burlington, Iowa, and St. Louis, followed in 1935. All were daytime trains. Then in November 1936 Burlington introduced its first new long-distance streamliner, the Budd-built *Denver Zephyr* between Chicago and Denver. Built of shining stainless steel, the *Denver Zephyr* was the fastest train in a part of America where *Zephyr* was quickly becoming a household name. It originally included five Budd sleeping cars in each of its two trainsets. This new train triggered a feud between Pullman and the Budd Company that would ultimately result in Pullman being embroiled in a federal anti-trust court case.

Pullman was hardly innocent. Prior to and during the *Denver Zephyr's* construction, Pullman was involved in contract re-negotiations with the Burlington to continue

RIGHT: The 1936 version of the stainless steel *Denver Zephyr* was a thing of beauty and one of the fastest trains in the world. Operating on an overnight run between Chicago and the Mile High City, the *DZ* helped establish the image of the streamliner as a fast, reliable and exciting form of travel. The train featured something unique at the time: sleeping cars built by somebody other than Pullman. Constructed of stainless steel by the Budd Company and owned by CB&Q (not Pullman), the cars were operated by Pullman under contract to CB&Q. The sleeping cars featured beautiful wood-walled interiors. JOE WELSH COLLECTION

operating that railroad's sleeping cars. Seeking to cast doubt on the product of its manufacturing competitor Budd, Pullman at first refused to operate Burlington sleeping cars not of Pullman manufacture. Explaining its actions, Pullman dug a deeper hole for itself. It claimed that the *Denver Zephyr's* Budd-built cars did not meet Pullman's high standards; Pullman even went so far as to require a "hold harmless" clause in its operating contract in the event of the structural failure of the Budd cars. Finally, and most damning, Pullman insisted that the Burlington buy no more than ten sleeping cars from Budd. Under pressure, and not wishing to incur the expense of operating

its own sleeping-car fleet (for Pullman had given Burlington an ultimatum), Burlington agreed.

A year later Pullman did exactly the same thing to the Santa Fe. Budd had built a wonderful, all-sleeping-car train for the railroad, the first streamlined *Super Chief* of 1937. Although the cars were absolutely beautiful, finished in fluted stainless steel outside and rare wood veneers and southwest Indian decor inside, Budd wouldn't get the chance to build any more sleeping cars for Santa Fe in the prewar years. Indeed, its share of the new sleeping-car market pre-war almost completely vanished. Pullman saw to that.

ABOVE: This is the car that started the feud that eventually ended in the court-ordered break up of Pullman. *Silver Skates*—a 12-section sleeper built by Budd, owned by CB&Q, and operated by Pullman—is shown at Denver on October 24, 1936. Pullman's strong-arm tactics with CB&Q to prevent the road from buying anymore sleepers from Budd led to a federal anti-trust action against Pullman. OTTO PERRY, DENVER PUBLIC LIBRARY, WESTERN HISTORY COLLECTION, IMAGE NO. OP-4868

As might be expected, Budd took exception to Pullman's behavior, and the federal government agreed. On July 12, 1940, the United States filed a civil suit in Philadelphia against Pullman under the Sherman Anti-Trust Act. Among other things, the complaint charged that The Pullman Company had a monopoly in the sleeping-car business. The government cited two major issues. Pullman had an exclusive-rights clause included in most of its operating agreements with railroads to provide all the sleeping-car service on those railroads. And, Pullman, therefore being the operator and purchaser of practically all the sleeping cars in the United States, ensured that a monopoly of sleeping-car construction contracts would go to its own manufacturing arm.

The fact that Pullman was on record as having strong-armed railroads into compliance at the direct expense of other builders didn't help. Neither did Pullman's image as a stodgy monopoly that resisted the inclusion of the modern products of builders like Budd. In point of fact, Pullman operated a higher percentage of streamlined cars in its fleet (5.6 percent) than the average railroad (3.7 percent) but the company couldn't seem to shake its image.

1933

FIRST LIGHTWEIGHT ALUMINUM SLEEPING CAR
The third great evolutionary milestone was reached when the first all-aluminum Pullman car was exhibited at A Century of Progress, Chicago, in 1933–34. A car with all the safety of steel but practically half the weight. Air-conditioning; indirect lighting; modified streamline effect and ingenious interior decorations were some of the outstanding advancements.

THE DRAWING ROOM WITH
MODERN PULLMAN COMFORTS

A BEAUTIFUL AND COMMODIOUS LOUNGE

1934

FIRST STREAMLINED SLEEPING CAR TRAIN
The first streamlined train with Pullman sleeping cars was operated in America in 1934 and broke all records for a transcontinental run from the Pacific to the Atlantic. The cars are of lightweight aluminum alloy construction with all the modern conveniences.

THE ENCLOSED PULLMAN SECTION—
A NEW FEATURE

PULLMAN ADOPTS THE STREAMLINER EFFECT
IN INTERIOR CONSTRUCTION

1937

FOLDING BED
AIR OUTLET
WARDROBE
WASHSTAND
HOPPER UNDER SEAT
SLIDING DOOR

FIRST LIGHTWEIGHT STREAMLINED "ROOMETTE" CAR
The "Roomette" car is lightweight, streamlined and constructed of high tensile alloy-steel by the welding process which gives a smooth exterior without rivet heads.

MIRROR
AIR OUTLET
WARDROBE
MIRROR LIGHTS
WASHSTAND
FOLDING BED NIGHT POSITION
SLIDING DOOR WITH MIRROR ON ROOM SIDE

THE ROOMETTE
PREPARED FOR DAYTIME OCCUPANCY

THE ROOMETTE
PREPARED FOR NIGHT TIME OCCUPANCY

This folder, which highlighted Pullman's notable developments during the 1930s, introduced the roomette to the general public. The accommodation was Pullman's most successful room design of the streamlined era. Eventually it would replace the section as Pullman's basic sleeping accommodation for one. The classic roomette would, in fact, survive to the twenty-first century on Amtrak.
PULLMAN, JOE WELSH COLLECTION

After a prolonged court proceeding, in May 1944 the federal government entered its final judgment. It required Pullman Incorporated to choose which business (sleeping-car operation or manufacturing) to keep and sell the other. Pullman's use of "exclusive rights clauses" was also declared illegal.

EXPANSION OF STREAMLINERS AND STREAMLINED PULLMANS

Before and during Pullman's landmark court battle, the company continued to build streamlined trains and operate streamlined sleeping cars. By 1940, Pullman was operating 388 lightweight sleepers, but it was still a relatively small

RIGHT: Union Pacific produced a whole series of small booklets to promote its passenger trains. Stylishly done art adorned the cover of the railroad's offering on the *Forty Niner*. Inside, the train's sleeping cars were described in detail. *UP, JOE WELSH COLLECTION*

BELOW: The *Forty Niner*'s cars may have been streamstyled outside, but on the inside, the train's three 12-section-drawing-room cars looked very similar to their un-streamlined brethren. *UNION PACIFIC RAILROAD MUSEUM, JOE WELSH COLLECTION*

percentage of Pullman's total fleet, and most of the lightweight cars operated on just a handful of the top trains in the nation. The average customer still experienced Pullman service in a heavyweight car.

But the lightweight Pullman fleet outgrew the undersized articulated trains of its birth to become full-sized, modern, non-articulated and truly attractive. Along the way in 1937, Pullman introduced one of the most significant accommodations in its history—the roomette. Designed to give individual patrons the privacy they longed for, it was a marvel of engineering. It featured a big picture window, a bed that folded down out of the wall, a toilet, washbasin, and clothes closet in a room

Text continued on page 80

ABOVE: In 1940, the Gulf, Mobile & Ohio Railroad introduced an overnight streamliner, the *Gulf Coast Rebel*, linking St. Louis and Mobile, Alabama. The train originally wore a silver-and-red livery by industrial designer Otto Kuhler. Each of the train's two equipment sets included a remodeled 8-section 1-drawing-room 3-double-bedroom sleeper incorporating Pullman's "Betterment" features such as a curved roof line, skirts, and modern interior appointments. The two cars, *Deep South* (depicted here in at Pullman's St. Louis shop in June 1946) Alton Railroad-GM&O merger colors of maroon and red) and *Show Me* were remodeled by Pullman's Calumet Shops from sleepers originally built in 1925. *PULLMAN, TRANSPORTATION COLLECTIONS, SMITHSONIAN INSTITUTION*

LEFT: Pullman was self-sufficient in just about every regard. Here, a worker re-upholsters seating. *PULLMAN, WILLIAM F. HOWES JR. COLLECTION*

Southern Pacific was a hotbed of prewar Pullman streamliners. Perhaps the most luxurious was the 1941 *Lark*, an overnight sleeper train between Los Angeles and San Francisco, with an Oakland section out of San Jose. Unlike its vibrant cousin streamliners, the red-and-orange *Daylight*s, the *Lark* wore a more subdued livery of two-tone gray. This edition of West, SP's employee magazine, featured the *Lark* on the cover and a "Five More!" cut line that referred to the two new *Lark* trainsets, two new *San Joaquin Daylight* trainsets, and a second set of equipment for the *City of San Francisco*. The advertising claimed the new *Lark* Pullmans cost some $80,000 each, versus about $35,000 for conventional Pullmans. The *Lark*'s overnight schedule made it a popular choice for Hollywood stars who wished to travel in luxury—and privacy.
KEVIN J. HOLLAND COLLECTION

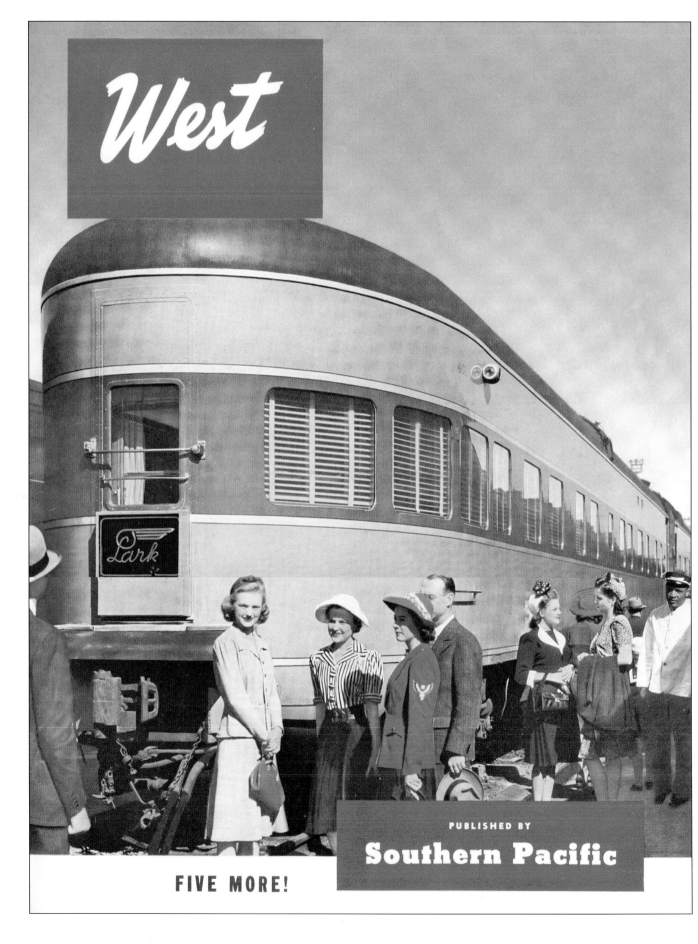

76

RIGHT: Originally the 12-section, 2-drawing-room *Costella Peak* built in the late 1920s for the *20th Century Limited*, *Rocket Tower* received its new name, streamlining, and silver paint, "Betterment Car" upgrades and an 8-section, 3-double-bedroom, 1-drawing-room configuration during a 1941 rebuild. Along with sister car *Zephyr Tower*, *Rocket Tower* was assigned to the St. Louis—Minneapolis *Zephyr Rocket,* operated jointly by the Rock Island and the Burlington. In 1948, *Rocket Tower* was purchased by the Rock Island and *Zephyr Tower* by the Burlington and leased back to Pullman. *HARRY STEGMAIER*

LEFT: Baltimore & Ohio's *Emerald Waters* reflects well the evolution of the steel heavyweight sleeping car. Built as the 16-section *Euclid* in 1918, it was remodeled in 1931 with 10 regular sections and 4 experimental private (enclosed) sections. In 1939, the car was rebuilt with 8 sections and 4 double bedrooms and upgraded to "Betterment Car" status with exterior streamlining (including skirting and full-width diaphragms), contemporary interior features, tightlock couplers, and an upgraded braking system. Renamed *Emerald Waters*, the car entered service on the B&O's premier Washington—Chicago run, the *Capitol Limited*. It was sold to the B&O in 1948, leased back to Pullman, further modernized, and used in various B&O and pool services until it was sold to the C. P. Huntington Chapter of the National Railway Historical Society in 1966. The car has been preserved and is currently on display at the B&O Railroad Museum in Baltimore. In this 1965 photograph, *Emerald Waters* is being switched by the Louisville & Nashville after arriving in Louisville on a Kentucky Derby Special. *HARRY STEGMAIER*

BELOW: Although built by Pullman-Standard in 1940 of lightweight construction, *Forest Canyon* had an 8-section, 5-double-bedroom floor plan more common to remodeled heavyweight cars of the 1930s. It was assigned to Rock Island's *Rocky Mountain Rocket*. *HARRY STEGMAIER*

ABOVE: Santa Fe's *Chief* between Chicago and Los Angeles was an all-Pullman train and one of the finest operations in the country. Streamlined in 1938, the *Chief* featured Pullman-built lightweight sleepers and sleeper-observation cars. Boarding at Chicago's Dearborn Station brought a first glimpse of the new train's stainless-steel Pullman observation car amidst the gloom of the train shed. *SANTA FE, JOE WELSH COLLECTION*

RIGHT: In addition to 4 drawing rooms and 2 double bedrooms, the 1938 *Chief*'s lightweight Pullman observation offered this inviting Art Deco lounge. *SANTA FE, JOE WELSH COLLECTION*

Immediately before and for a time after World War II, the majority of Pullman cars in service were still heavyweight cars. In this poignant view taken circa 1941, the Chicago & Eastern Illinois *Zipper* departs the train shed of Chicago's Dearborn Station on its journey to St. Louis. The train's consist has been shortened by competition from the Alton, Wabash and Illinois Central, but the *Zipper* still carries a 20-seat Pullman parlor observation in the *Empress* prefix series on its rear, its platform railing adorned with a drumhead advertising the train. On the left is Santa Fe's streamlined, all-Pullman *Chief. BIG FOUR GRAPHICS*

ABOVE: Built by Pullman-Standard for *Chief* service in 1938, *Tolchico* and its 13 sister cars each contained 8 sections, 2 bedrooms, and 2 compartments. A new innovation, upper-bed positions in both the sections and compartments had small windows. Riding on its prewar trucks, the car is show, still in active service, in 1965. *ALAN BRADLEY*

RIGHT: This Pullman drawing room, shown with the lower berth made down for the evening, was Pullman's premium accommodation offered on the 1938 *Chief*. The train and its counterpart, the *Super Chief*, handled their share of Hollywood celebrities over the years. *SANTA FE, JOE WELSH COLLECTION*

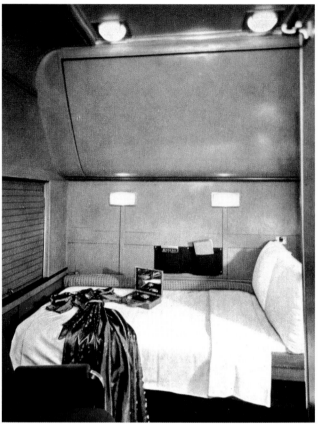

Text continued from page 74

with permanent walls and a sliding door for complete privacy. The roomette was the logical replacement for the single occupancy section as Pullman's standard accommodation for one. Introduced experimentally in 1937, the roomette was demonstrated in cars *Roomette I* and *Roomette II* which ran on a variety of railroads. The accommodation, along with the double bedroom, would form the backbone of new non-articulated streamlined cars featured primarily on Pullman-built and operated lightweight trains. These included such famous name trains as the *20th Century Limited* (New York Central, 1938), the *Broadway Limited* (Pennsylvania Railroad, 1938), the *Chief* (Santa Fe, 1938), the *Lark* (Southern Pacific, 1941) and others.

Rebuilt trains and cars also offered Pullman accommodations. Some heavyweight Pullman cars were remodeled to appear to be streamlined. These cars typically operated together with true lightweight cars in upgraded trains on railroads such as the Pennsylvania (the Fleet of Modernism trains of 1938) or Union Pacific (*Forty Niner*, 1937) or in entirely rebuilt trains (Baltimore & Ohio's *Capitol Limited*,1938, and *National Limited*, 1940).

The new lightweight streamliners and remodeled heavyweight trains boosted ridership or, at the very least, helped their railroads' marketing image. It appeared that the trend toward adding new streamliners would continue unabated, but World War II interrupted suddenly in December 1941.

WARTIME

As a result of war, the construction of streamliners ceased. Beginning in 1940 a shortage of Cor-Ten steel occurred as a result of U.S. concerns about the war in Europe. All the exotic metals used to create streamlined cars could be put to better use in military applications. Illinois Central's *Panama Limited*, inaugurated as a lightweight train on May 1, 1942, between Chicago and New Orleans, was the last luxury all-Pullman streamliner introduced after Pearl Harbor. (IC had in fact been ordered to cease production of the train, but the railroad argued that its two new *Panama* trainsets would increase the railroad's capacity to carry soldiers.) The very last new streamliner introduced (on June 21, 1942) was Missouri Pacific's *Colorado Eagle*, a coach-and-sleeper train that included lightweight Pullman-built sleeping cars with 6 sections, 6 roomettes, and 4 double bedrooms. A small number of other individual Pullman-built lightweight car orders, placed before the war, trickled in to a handful of railroads. But after October 1943, no more Pullman-built cars would be delivered to the railroads until 1946.

Pullman's mission changed, too. It had always been a keystone of the American civilian passenger transport network; now, as in World War I, it became a vital cog in the war machine. Rail passenger transportation expanded dramatically as a result of war. Many railroads experienced a fourfold increase in their passenger traffic during the conflict and some like the Norfolk & Western which served the major navy and civilian port of Norfolk, Virginia, saw their passenger traffic increase elevenfold!

Like the railroads it ran on, Pullman handled an amazing amount of traffic during World War II. All told, including troops, it was estimated that 125 million passengers traveled 98 billion miles in Pullman cars during the conflict. To put this incredible demand in perspective, consider that the total population of the United States was 131 million in 1945.

This extra burden significantly impacted the way Pullman served the general public. Not only was it important for Pullman to remind its civilian customers to travel only if it were necessary, but the company also had to explain to the public why they might not be able to find any Pullman space on board.

During the conflict, the government set the ground rules and priorities for the railroads and Pullman through the Office of Defense Transportation. Although control of the railroads and Pullman remained in private hands, the ODT set regulations aimed at conserving capacity to move troops.

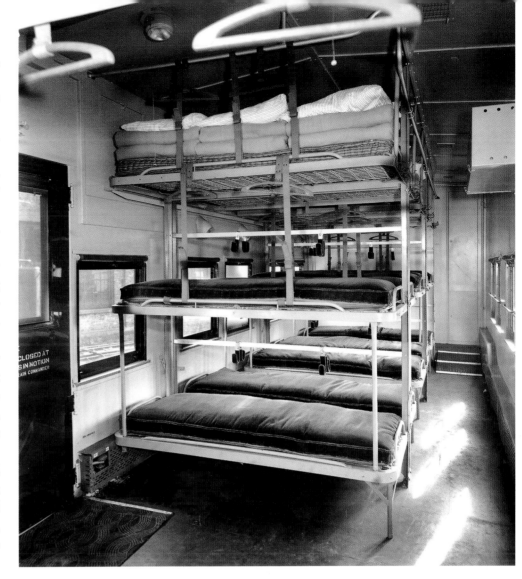

ABOVE: Although working under difficult conditions, Pullman attempted to maintain its traditional service standards aboard troop cars. The porter has prepared these three-tiered berths for night occupancy by 29 soldiers and himself. *SMITHSONIAN INSTITUTION*

LEFT: In addition to the hundreds of sleepers reassigned or remodeled to respond to the unprecedented transportation demands of World War II, Pullman built 2,400 troop sleepers in two lots of 1,200 cars each. The cars were owned by the Federal government's Defense Plant Corporation and operated under contract by Pullman. Although appearing to be little more than a boxcar with windows, each sleeper accommodated 29 troops and a Pullman porter with a modicum of comfort on 10 rows of seats that converted into three-tiered berths at night. The cars rode on trucks capable of passenger-train speeds. Following the war, they found alternate uses including as maintenance-of-way equipment and conversion to baggage, mail, and express cars. *WILLIAM F. HOWES JR. COLLECTION*

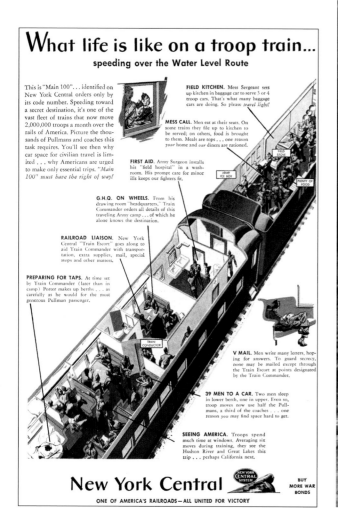

ABOVE: In the 1940s, New York Central ran a series of magazine ads that showed behind-the-scenes workings of passenger-train travel, including this depiction of life aboard a troop train. This ad appeared in the September 1943 National Geographic.—*WILLIAM F. HOWES JR. COLLECTION*

ABOVE RIGHT: Pullman carried millions of troops in World War II. Some traveled in older heavyweight Pullman cars while others rode in newly constructed troop sleepers. In a driving rain, soldiers board a troop sleeper on the Union Pacific. *UNION PACIFIC RAILROAD MUSEUM, IMAGE NO. N1326-2, JOE WELSH COLLECTION*

In October 1942, ODT General Order No. 24 "froze" passenger train service, requiring an ODT permit to operate extra trains or extra sections of existing trains. The effect of the order was to severely curtail seasonal (read, vacation-oriented) trains such as those serving Florida on winter-only schedules. The goal was to free up the Pullman pool for troop movements.

That pool consisted of thousands of rebuilt regular heavyweights and tourist cars. To augment this fleet, Pullman-Standard Car Manufacturing, now temporarily owned by the Defense Plant Corporation, turned out 1,200 new troop sleepers. Resembling box cars, the troop sleepers included very basic accommodations, including triple-tiered bunks, a feature once offered by Pullman in its prewar failed experiment, the coach-sleeper. An additional 88 obsolete Pullman cars were converted to hospital cars, some with full operating rooms, to transport injured troops. Eventually some of these cars also performed the sad duty of carrying the remains of soldiers. During the war, the veteran Pullman car fleet and new Pullman troop sleepers handled 33 million service personnel who traveled 44 billion miles in special troop movements. These movements were hauled by the railroads but organized and scheduled by the Army Transportation Corps.

The railroads and Pullman experienced their highest war demand in 1945. The U.S. and its allies had been fighting a two-front war, in Europe and the Pacific. Germany's surrender in May 1945 allowed the Allied Force to shift its undivided attention to conquering Japan. To do so, it was anticipated that the millions of combatants accumulated in Europe over the past four years would have to be shifted to the Pacific theater in just ten months. Most would have to cross the country in Pullman cars.

To support this anticipated increase in troop movements, the ODT issued two other orders that affected

Pullman operations. In January 1945, the ODT further restricted the operation of seasonal trains to any resort or vacation area. A more significant impact occurred in mid July 1945 when another ODT order prohibited the operation of sleeping cars by any railroad to destinations under 450 miles from the point of origin of the cars. As a result of the order, the Pennsylvania Railroad withdrew 159 Pullman sleeping cars from service and temporarily discontinued its all-Pullman overnight train between New York and Pittsburgh, the *Pittsburgher*, before reintroducing it as a late afternoon train without sleepers. The New Haven's famous overnight *Owl* between New York and Boston had its Pullman sleeping cars replaced by parlor cars where it was hoped late-night patrons could still stretch out in some form of comfort.

Japan's sudden surrender in September 1945 presented an even greater challenge. Over 5.5 million veterans would return from overseas between November 1945 and June 1946. Waiting to take them home were approximately 4,200 Pullman sleepers and 1,200 Pullman troop sleepers. It was the largest single purpose movement of people in Pullman history.

Socially, Pullman became a part of the war experience for many Americans. The most famous railroad advertisement of the war, the New Haven Railroad's "The Kid in Upper 4", featured a nervous boy heading away from home and off to war in a Pullman berth. For millions of Americans, including some who died, the ride into and out of the fight started and ended in a Pullman car. And for those left behind, Pullman often provided the first or last glimpse of a loved one.

Pullman employees also bore the brunt of war. It wasn't easy to take care of a car full of battle weary GIs or raw recruits. And for Pullman's Filipino car attendants assigned to club and lounge car service, there was the added difficulty of being mistaken for Japanese.

The war taxed Pullman like never before. But the future would offer little respite. Ahead lay a forced reorganization of the company and overwhelming competition from the automobile and the airplane. Pullman's (and the railroads') reward for helping win the war was the government turning its back on the railroad industry. In the next decade the federal government would significantly subsidize airlines, highways, and waterways, and Pullman would be an early victim of a fundamental shift in the way Americans traveled.

One of the more memorable World War II advertisements was New Haven's "The Kid in Upper 4", appearing in the December 21, 1942, edition of *Life* Magazine.—*WILLIAM F. HOWES JR. COLLECTION*

With today's 600-miles-per-hour air travel interrupted by airport security hassles, high-speed highways snarled with urban traffic, and instant access to the knowledge via the internet, it's tempting to reflect on a time a half a century or so ago when life seemed to move at a much easier pace. It was just before the dawn of commercial jet aviation and the Defense Highway System (the Interstate). Many travelers still preferred the all-weather safety, reliability, and comfort of the railroad passenger train. This often meant booking space aboard the parlor and sleeping cars of The Pullman Company.

America's railroads had emerged from World War II acutely aware of the growing threat of improved air and highway transportation. "But, getting there by train is half the fun of any trip!" became the rallying cry of rail-travel advocates in the face of this competition. Although the railroads had been severely limited in their ability to acquire new equipment during the Great Depression of the 1930s and World War II, the enthusiastic public response to the few streamliners that were built just before the war prompted the industry to invest heavily following the conflict. This included the purchase of new sleeping, parlor, dining, and lounge cars that catered to the business and upscale vacation traveler, both types being longtime Pullman mainstays.

Heavyweight parlor-car service, like this shown on New Haven's *Yankee Clipper* between New York and Boston, was a veritable private club on wheels.
MITCH MARKOVITZ ILLUSTRATION

But new postwar trains were slow in coming due to a backlog of car orders. So, for the next decade, one could still experience the traditional comforts of the heavyweight or "standard" equipment of the 1920s as well as the glamour and excitement of the new streamliners.

SHORT-HAUL SERVICE: PARLOR TRAVEL AND SET-OUT SLEEPERS

Imagine Pullman travel from that time. It's the spring of 1956. Living with your family in suburban Baltimore, you commute on the Baltimore & Ohio Railroad to a Washington, D.C., office in the shadow of Dwight D. Eisenhower's White House. You've been asked to make a business trip to New York City. Since the meeting is in midtown Manhattan, you opt for the train. Your office subscribes to the *Official Guide of the Railways*, so it's an easy task to investigate alternative routes and schedules.

The day of your trip has been hectic, and there's no way you'll make B&O's *Royal Blue* or Pennsylvania Railroad's *Afternoon Congressional*, nor any of the approximately hourly services scheduled through the early evening. If lucky, you might just catch the Pennsylvania's *Potomac* leaving at 9:30 p.m. The good news: The *Guide* informs that, although the railroad apparently feels no need to operate a dining car on this late-evening train, the *Potomac* does carry a Pullman parlor-buffet-lounge car offering dinner for first-class passengers. You'll try for a parlor seat if you get to station in time.

Passing between the tall, white columns of Washington's Union Station just after 8:40 p.m., you head for the ticket counter and ask, "Is a parlor car seat available on the Pennsy's 9:30 to New York?" The clerk calls the terminal's diagram room. Here, 3 x 12-inch forms printed on light cardstock, called "diagrams," are used to maintain a handwritten record of current ticket sales and future reservations for accommodations in sleepers, parlor cars, and coaches where space is assigned in advance. Pullman has designated a "line number" for each scheduled service it operates. A train may have one or more Pullman "lines," each filled with a particular car type. Each type has a unique diagram form, identified by a "diagram number," showing individually all the accommodations in that car. The railroad has assigned a "loading number" for each reserved-accommodation car on a train. The individual seat or room accommodations have been distributed among one or more space-assigning offices, usually either a central reservation bureau or at cities generating a significant amount of traffic for that train. Each of these offices maintains on its diagrams a reservation and sale record for the space it controls. On the day the train operates, the diagrams for Pullman cars in that trip's consist are given to the Pullman staff aboard to reconcile the assignment offices' information with the tickets actually presented by passengers. Since diagrams are typically maintained for each day a car line will operate over a three-month period, larger offices, such as this one in Union Station, have several thousand active diagrams on hand at all times.

The answer to your inquiry tonight is "affirmative," and you are assigned seat 10 aboard car 500 on Pennsylvania Railroad train No. 150, the *Potomac*, to New York. The ticket clerk issues you two tickets, one in the amount of $11.06 (including 10 percent federal tax) reflecting the first-class fare on the PRR from Washington to New York and the other covering the Pullman Company's charge of $2.30 (including tax) for occupancy of a seat in the parlor car it is operating under contract with the Pennsylvania. The serial number on the Pullman ticket is communicated to the diagram room for entry on the diagram for car 500 in the space labeled "Seat 10." You check the tickets and charge the total amount to your Rail Travel Card, a new credit arrangement subscribed to by most railroads.

Diagram cards depict the general configuration of the accommodations in each type of car in which accommodations can be reserved in advance. Each ticketing location holding space for sale maintains a manual record of transactions involving that sale. *THE PULLMAN COMPANY, MIKE SCHAFER COLLECTION*

THE PULLMAN COMPANY — DIAGRAM Form 207-D

8 DUPLEX-ROOMETTES 6 ROOMETTES 4 DOUBLE BEDROOMS

* Mark for Advance Preparation. A One Berth. B Two Berths.
E No Advance Preparation. Bracketed Duplex-Roomettes are Opposite.
Connecting Rooms: (A & B) and (C & D).

* DOUBLE BEDROOM D — Crosswise Sofa Bed and Upper
* DOUBLE BEDROOM C — Lengthwise Sofa Seat Folding Bed and Upper
* DOUBLE BEDROOM B — Lengthwise Sofa Seat Folding Bed and Upper
* DOUBLE BEDROOM A — Crosswise Sofa Bed and Upper

DUPLEX-ROOMETTES

UPPER DUPLEX-ROOMETTES	LOWER DUPLEX-ROOMETTES
DUPLEX-ROOMETTE 14	DUPLEX-ROOMETTE 12
DUPLEX-ROOMETTE 13	DUPLEX-ROOMETTE 11
DUPLEX-ROOMETTE 10	DUPLEX-ROOMETTE 8
DUPLEX-ROOMETTE 9	DUPLEX-ROOMETTE 7

ROOMETTES

ROOMETTE 5	ROOMETTE 6
ROOMETTE 3	ROOMETTE 4
ROOMETTE 1	ROOMETTE 2

CAR   LINE
TRAIN No.   LEAVE
FROM   TO
DAY   DATE

For many years, The Pullman Company has used ticket stock in some 14 different colors to distinguish between it's various types of accommodations and service; for example, pink for a lower berth, yellow for an upper, and so forth. But recently, some railroads have been trying book-style or even office-machine-produced tickets, and Pullman is adapting.

As you wait on the concourse for your train to be called for boarding, the Pullman attendant for car 500 is obtaining a copy of the diagram identifying which seats in his car will be occupied, the associated ticket numbers or reservation codes, and where his passengers will be boarding and leaving the train. The diagram office has also specified certain unsold seats that may be sold on the train, as well as others it has just transferred to stations up the line to cover last minute sales.

Boarding begins about 9:10 p.m. and passengers, some with Red Cap porters assisting with luggage, stream down the platform aside the Tuscan red cars of Pennsylvania's *Potomac*. Parlor car 500 is identified by a lighted sign (whose number can be changed to reflect the assigned loading number for the trip at hand) in the window adjacent to an open door. Your home for the next four hours dates from 1929 and still proudly displays the name *Friars Club*. A Filipino attendant in white jacket and black bow tie greets you, takes your bag, assists you up the car's steps, and guides you to seat 10 in a warmly lit room of 12 deep-cushioned wing chairs, each adjacent to a partially shaded window and designed to rotate to positions comfortable for either privacy, conversation with fellow passengers, viewing passing scenery, or the use of a small drop table located under the window. The attendant has already stored your bag in a closet near the car's entrance and now offers to take your coat and hat and place them in an overhead rack. You've barely settled in when the GG1 electric locomotive up front eases the train smoothly out of the station. The brightly lit U.S. Capitol dome recedes into the night.

Before the *Potomac* hits its stride at 80 miles per hour, the Pullman attendant, diagram in hand, and the PRR conductor arrive to take tickets. There being only one Pullman car in operation on train 150 out of Washington this evening, the company does not need to assign its own conductor to the run. Rather, the car's attendant is in charge. He is assisted with the meal and beverage services aboard the car by a bus boy.

Although the attendant offers to bring a drink, your focus now is on dinner. Just past a small kitchen, you enter an area of six tables, each with four chairs, set with white linens and heavy, plated silverware. Beyond is a lounge with inward-facing chairs and settees beside

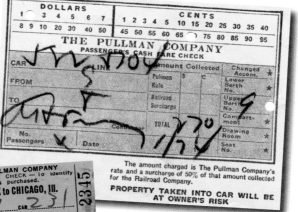

chrome-plated smoking stands with trays on which to rest drinks. This car's features are certainly more diverse than the typical parlor car with its rows of individual, rotating seats and, perhaps, a private drawing room with sofas and chairs for groups of up to five people. Some postwar parlor cars on the New Haven Railroad also have day roomettes with two facing seats, making them ideal for one or two people. You've used these private accommodations when traveling with business associates or your family, taking advantage of the portable tables that can be readily installed for work, games, or meals.

Once you've been seated in the dining room by the attendant, and as the area fills up, he asks if he can seat another passenger at your table. This is a tradition on the railroad where space is at a premium, so you agree. Furthermore, you've found it can result in a stimulating conversation that makes the trip pass more quickly.

The menu is limited to mostly light meals, but it does feature a small charcoal-grilled sirloin steak on toast points, served with grilled sliced Spanish onions and potatoes. This is accompanied by tomato on a bed of lettuce and Guildmaster Sauce. You order the steak, plus a Cuba Libre, while your table mate selects Pullman's popular chilled salmon plate and a glass of Grant's Best Procurable

FACING PAGE: Dining aboard a Pullman restaurant or dinette car was an experience not to be forgotten. Pictured here is the *Mariner* in assignment to the Pere Marquette Railway. Similar cars were assigned to the Pennsylvania Railroad. The china is of the "Indian Tree" pattern and delicacies like double lamb chops or sirloin steak are on the menu. *MITCH MARKOVITZ ILLUSTRATION*

INSET: Paper, not computers, in the form of receipts such as these was how Pullman ticketing, accommodations, sales, and other transactions were tracked for both Pullman itself and the customer. *MIKE SCHAFER COLLECTION*

whiskey, "on-the-rocks." The meals arrive on china with Pullman's distinctive orange-flowered "Indian Tree" design. Your tab comes to $3.50; his to $1.95.

After dinner, the lounge beckons for a Drambuie and a smoke. Unfortunately, your cigarettes are back at the office, so you select a pack of Herbert Tareyton's from Pullman's extensive offerings.

The car nearly empties at Philadelphia. You head back to your easy chair for the post-midnight dash into New York. Outside it's pitch black; inside, the incandescent yellow beams from wall sconces, table lamps, and dimmed bulbs in the clerestory are quickly absorbed into the room's dark walls and fabrics. It's perfect for dozing. You're awakened by a blast of air outside the car as the *Potomac* plunges into the tunnels under the Hudson River. While the *Friars Club* trails through the switches entering Pennsylvania Station, its attendant offers to brush off any dust that may

ABOVE: A welcome complimentary service aboard overnight trains catering largely to business travelers was the train secretary. The positions were filled by men with stenographic skills and employed by either the railroad or Pullman. In addition to taking dictation and typing letters, the train secretaries handled telegrams to and from passengers while en route. The secretary depicted here is aboard B&O's *Capitol Limited.* By the late 1950s, the clientele and needs for these services had largely evaporated and the positions were abolished. BALTIMORE & OHIO, WILLIAM F. HOWES JR. COLLECTION

RIGHT: The services of a Pullman maid-manicurist were available on some of America's premier trains. In the mid-1920s, Pullman employed more than 200 women in this role to tend principally to the needs of women and children. By the 1950s, that function, among others, was being performed by stewardess-nurses employed by some railroads. BALTIMORE & OHIO, WILLIAM F. HOWES JR. COLLECTION

The most basic and common of Pullman accommodations was the section, with its upper and lower berths shown here as prepared for night occupancy. Over 90 percent of Pullman's heavyweight cars had at least some sections, and, the accommodation was still to be found on many lightweight trains right up to the day Pullman ceased operating sleepers in 1968. A section was formed by a pair of facing seats that could be converted into a lower berth, upon which a mattress was placed. Above the seats, hinged to the outer wall of the car, an upper berth could be lowered into place. Access to the upper berth was by a ladder, and security against rolling out of bed was provided by safety net. Amenities included a mirror; bracket for a portable table; reading and night lights; hangers, hammocks, and shelves for clothing and small items; crisp, clean linens; soft pillows and warm blankets. Sleeping passengers were shielded from the aisle by heavy curtains. And at the push of a call button, an expertly trained porter was on hand to assist you. *JOHN DUBAS, WILLIAM F. HOWES JR. COLLECTION*

Operating prior to the computer and internet age, Pullman reservations were made by telephone or in person at a railroad station or a railroad's city ticket office. The reservation was tracked on a paper car diagram. Note the numerous public timetables on the racks in the background. *THE PULLMAN COMPANY, WILLIAM F. HOWES JR. COLLECTION*

have accumulated on your clothes en route. He places your bags on the high-level platform. A 25-cent tip (in addition to that given with meal and bar bills) is considered standard for this run. You accept the Red Cap's offer to take your bags through the station's concourse of soaring steel and glass canopies to the taxi stand. One of New York's omnipresent Checker cabs takes less than 10 minutes to deliver you to the Hotel Commodore adjacent to Grand Central Terminal at 42nd Street and Lexington Avenue. You're only a quick cab ride away from the location of tomorrow's business meeting.

You had originally planned to catch an afternoon train back to Baltimore after completing your business, but "My Fair Lady" is playing on Broadway and you have a ticket! The overnight "set-out" sleeper services offered by both the PRR and B&O to Baltimore would allow you to have dinner and attend the show, board a Pullman anytime after 10 p.m. (10:30 on the Pennsy), stay aboard in Baltimore until 8 a.m., and still be home in time for breakfast. Although the B&O train's departure from the

Jersey Central Railroad's terminal across the Hudson River in Jersey City, New Jersey, is less convenient than the Pennsylvania's at its Manhattan station, you have always enjoyed the ferryboat ride across the Hudson River. A visit to B&O's 42nd Street ticket office, and the clerk's quick call to the Jersey City diagram room, yields railroad and Pullman tickets for lower berth 2 in car 111 on B&O train No. 11, the St. Louis-bound *Metropolitan Special*, departing Jersey City at 12:50 a.m., with placement of your car in Baltimore at 5:55 a.m. B&O motorcoaches collect passengers at various Manhattan hotels and other locations for transport on the Jersey Central's Liberty Street ferry to train side at the Jersey City Terminal. Since the 42nd Street bus stop is convenient to your hotel and the theater, and you can check your baggage directly to your Pullman accommodation, you decide to use one of the evening's several bus runs from there to train 11.

The show was great, and now you're on B&O's 11:05 p.m. bus being floated across the Hudson on the Jersey Central ferry *Elizabeth*. (Actually, the bus driver has let you out on deck to enjoy the glittering lights of New York's nighttime skyline.)

A receiving table is set up at the Jersey City Terminal where a Pullman conductor, armed with the diagrams for the three sleepers on tonight's *Metropolitan Special*, is joined by the railroad's conductor in collecting tickets and reconciling any problems with duplicate sales and other space-assignment issues. The Pullman conductor notes that the upper berth in section 2 has not been sold and suggests that, for just $1.55, you can upgrade to a single-occupancy section (SOS), wherein the upper berth will be raised to afford more room for dressing and its mattress used to supplement that of your lower berth. Although this is only a modest addition to Pullman's $5 charge for a lower berth, you decide the extra amenities are not needed on such a short trip.

In addition to the Baltimore set-out car, the *Metropolitan Special* carries sleepers destined to Washington, D.C., and St. Louis. All are heavyweight cars built prior to 1930 but subsequently modernized with various mechanical betterments including air-conditioning and, in some cases, modest streamlining. Open sections with upper and lower berths predominate, although some private rooms are also offered. In conversations on the bus, you learned that among your fellow travelers are several officials with the Kelly-Springfield Tire Company of Cumberland, Maryland, and the West Virginia Pulp & Paper Company near Piedmont, West Virginia, plus a dean from Ohio University in Athens, Ohio. For them, flying is not a viable alternative.

Tickets collected, you proceed to car 111, tonight the *Garden Brook* in B&O's regal blue-and-gray paint scheme. The African-American porter leads you down a dimly lit aisle of heavy, dark green curtains, finally pulling one back to reveal lower 2. Given the late hour, he has already made down the berth, figuring you'll want to go right to bed. The crisp white linens, two pillows, and cedar-colored wool blanket with a "Pullman" monogram identifying your host for the night, invite slumber. A small sign posted at the end of the car stating that "QUIET is Requested for the Benefit of Those Who Have Retired" reminds you that many of the berths have already been occupied for almost three hours. In addition to the car's eight open sections, there are five double bedrooms, each with a sofa that converts to a lower berth and an upper berth that folds down from the ceiling. The rooms have individual washbasin and toilet facilities. There is a familiar, strangely comforting, mustiness to the *Garden Brook* that speaks to its advanced age and more than a million miles of safe travel.

Once the porter has stowed your bags and recorded on his "call card" a request for a 7 a.m. wake up, you adjourn to a communal men's washroom at the far end of the car. This also serves as a smoking lounge and place for male passengers from the sections to congregate. Here, veteran travelers and con artists have long regaled naive passengers with tall tales. Women, of course, have a similar, though hopefully more refined, facility.

Back at lower 2, you proceed through the acrobatics of getting ready for bed behind the curtains that shield you and your berth from the rest of the car. And, once again you marvel at the ingenuity of George M. Pullman, his peers, and successors in designing this most basic—and sometimes rather challenging—component of the railway sleeping car: the section. Within just 21 square

feet of floor space there is found, by day, two facing sofa-seats, each with an adjustable back and headrest, individual reading lights, air-flow controls, a mirror, ash trays, and provisions for setting up a table. Under Pullman's protocol, the passenger who has purchased the lower berth gets to ride forward. By night, this space transforms into upper and lower berths, each with a comfortable mattress, bedding, hangers, and hammocks or shelves for storing clothes and small articles. And upon the push of a call button, there is a porter ready to assist.

You consider a lower berth to be quite comfortable and, while in motion, enjoy raising a window shade a bit to watch the night scene pass by. By contrast, you find the climb up a ladder and into an upper berth to be awkward, and the windowless space to be claustrophobic. It's no wonder that so many uppers are vacant these days!

The last order of business before turning out the lights is to lay out tomorrow's clothes on the convenient shelf formed by the seatback's adjustable headrest and put your shoes under the berth for the porter to retrieve, shine, and replace during the night. All too soon, the porter's slight tug on the curtain, accompanied by a soft "Good morning, lower 2, it's seven o'clock," alerts you to the fact that *Garden Brook* is now standing by itself at Baltimore's Camden Station. Another comfortable trip in a Pullman has come to an end.

LONG-DISTANCE PULLMAN TRAVEL

You have hardly had a chance to enjoy Washington's spring weather before you are making plans for a Chicago visit in early May. Flying has become an increasingly desirable option in recent years, but the threat of bad weather in the Midwest gives cause for concern. And you have to admit you've become a creature of habit when it comes to traveling to Chicago. Both the Pennsylvania's Washington–Chicago *Liberty Limited* and B&O's Jersey City–Washington–Chicago *Capitol Limited* are top-notch operations. So, the train it will be. And since you can park at B&O's Silver Spring, Maryland, station in

Continued on page 96

A conductor's pouch with passenger receipt, for tickets collected for each parlor or sleeping-car accommodation.
MIKE SCHAFER COLLECTION

L Nº 155143

NOTICE TO PASSENGERS
Retain this Check until unused portion of Railroad equivalent is Returned
SEE THAT RETURN IS MADE BEFORE LEAVING THE CAR

20M 6-63   FORM 101

L Nº 155143

BALTIMORE & OHIO RAILROAD
Car No. *111*

No. of Seat or Berth Occupied
Seat
Upper
Lower *2*
Room

On car at *Jersey City*
Will leave car at *Baltimore*

INCLOSURE	TICKET No.		TICKET No.
	Local O. W.	S. T.	
	60 Day R. T.	S. L. S. T.	
State Consecutive	30 Day R. T.	W. T.	
Number	15 Day R. T.	S. L. W. T.	
	6 Mos.	Clergy	
	A. Y. T.	Scrip	
	Intl. O. W.	Other Kind	
		Passes	

B&O's all-Pullman *Capitol Limited* glides eastward along the Potomac River near Harpers Ferry, West Virginia., circa 1937, shortly after new Electro-Motive diesel-electric locomotives were assigned to the Chicago–Washington–Jersey City flagship, the first phase of streamlining for this famous train. The heavyweight cars partially visible here will soon be relegated to other duties as modernized heavyweight sleepers (facing page), rebuilt by B&O's Mount Royal Shops, are reintroduced as streamlined equipment. *BALTIMORE & OHIO, MIKE SCHAFER COLLECTION*

ABOVE: *Green Bank* was a heavyweight 12-section 1-drawing-room Pullman given a streamlined appearance at B&O's Mount Royal Shops (background) in 1938 for assignment to the *Capitol Limited*. It wears designer Otto Kuhler's stylish paint scheme of dark blue with a gray window band and gray along the edge of the roof. Gold pin striping and lettering complete the look. In later years, as the *Capitol* was upgraded with still newer cars, *Green Bank* was relegated to secondary runs like the *Metropolitan Special*. PULLMAN COMPANY, TRANSPORT HISTORY PRESS, JOE WELSH COLLECTION

BELOW: As newly modernized cars rolled forth from B&O's Mount Royal Shops, they were integrated into the equipment pool for the all-Pullman *Capitol Limited*. Eventually, all consists (three were necessary to protect the *Capitol*'s daily departures from Jersey City, Washington and Chicago) were fully streamlined, resulting in one of the most handsome "new" streamliners of the pre-World War II era. In the charge of new Electro-Motive EA locomotives and its streamlining completed, the *Capitol* leaves behind the hazy skyline of Chicago circa 1938. TOM MARTORANO, MIKE SCHAFER COLLECTION

A major part of your Pullman trip was the services of a professional crew. In the images in this series (counterclockwise from photo at right):

1. The conductor greets each passenger who has just boarded to verify the reservation and that he or she is in the correct accommodation.

2. While carrying your bags, the porter leads you to your accommodation and stows the baggage.

3. Once at your room, the porter explains the features such as temperature control, light switches, and call buttons.

4. When you're ready to turn in for the night, a press of the call button brings the porter to your room. While you head for the lounge for a nightcap, he makes down the bed.

5. While you sleep the night away, the porter is tends to various duties; one of the services entails polishing your shoes, which you have left in a special compact locker in your room; the locker is accessible from outside in the corridor.

6. Your shoes being polished for your next day's business meeting in Cleveland (or Chicago or New York or Los Angeles).

7. Both conductor and porter have paperwork to tend to, including marking up defects (burned out lamps, punctured seat cushions, etc.) that will need to be addressed by service crews during the car's layover at a terminal. Such paperwork can also include wake-up calls for the customer.

ALL PHOTOS, THE PULLMAN COMPANY, WILLIAM F. HOWES JR. COLLECTION

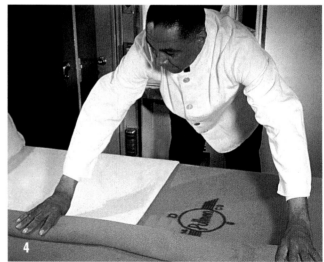

Continued from page 93

suburban Washington, the *Capitol Limited* is the logical choice for this trip.

You've been planning to try the *Capitol Limited's* newest accommodation, the duplex roomette. It's a private room costing only about 10 percent more than a lower berth. Two cars with these rooms operate to Chicago nightly; one originating in Washington, the other in Jersey City. As usual when traveling B&O, you call the road's Washington City Ticket Office (CTO) on "H" Street at Connecticut Avenue. The agent's quick check of the diagram room at Washington Union Station reveals that the westbound Washington car is sold out. Knowing that railroad offices in Jersey City, Philadelphia, Wilmington and Baltimore have each been assigned certain duplex roomettes in the car originating in Jersey City, he advises you the CTO will wire or call these locations in search of space. Later in the day, an exchange of wires with Philadelphia determines that of the three duplex roomettes held by that office, one, No 8, is available and will be kept, pending completion of the sale and ticketing, under a reservation code from the Washington CTO. Every office in the country selling Pullman space has been assigned a two or three-letter code. The code for B&O's Washington City Ticket Office is "WB." This, plus a sequential reservation transaction number, identifies the office making the reservation and the specific transaction. The CTO has notified Philadelphia that your reservation should be held under "WB254." Philadelphia has entered that information, along with the hold limit date for completing the sale and the note "On at Silver Spring" in the space for duplex roomette 8 on its diagram for car 58 of the date of your departure.

As for your return from Chicago, the diagram room at Washington Union Station holds two open sections and nine private rooms—including two duplex roomettes— on the eastbound *Capitol Limited*. This often expedites the handling of round-trip requests. Their duplex roomette 7 in car 65 was available. Being local to Union Station, B&O's CTO was immediately able to secure this space by telephone and have it held under your name until ticketed, without the requirement for a reservation code.

Once the CTO notifies you that all your Pullman space has been secured, you'll stop by during a lunch hour to pick up your tickets. The ticket for your westbound room will include the notation "reservation code WB254" so the conductor can compare it with Philadelphia's entry for duplex roomette 8 on their diagram for car 58. The CTO will also give the diagram room at Union Station the serial number on the Pullman ticket they issued for duplex roomette 7 in eastbound car 65 for entry onto the diagram for that car. The same information will be given to Chicago to be included on the car 65 diagram being provided to the Pullman conductor.

The day of your departure has arrived, and you are on the Silver Spring platform when B&O No 5, the *Capitol Limited*, pulls in at 5:43 p.m. You're standing at the location where the station announcer said car 58 would stop and, indeed, it has, with its porter ready to assist you aboard. In fact, he's been expecting you, having reviewed

7

5

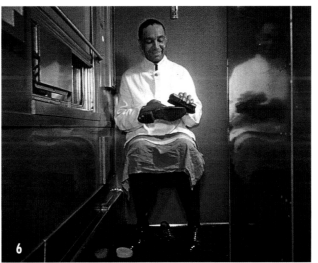

6

Early on, the Pennsylvania Railroad urged Pullman to design a new type of sleeper that catered to individual travelers wanting economical private rooms. The trick was for Pullman to come up with a floor plan that featured the high capacity of a section sleeper but with private-room accommodations. The answer was to stagger compact rooms in a split-level format. Shown in August 1962, *Major Brook* was an early streamlined car featuring this "duplex" arrangement of staggered room levels. *Major Brook* and its nine sister cars, all with *Brook* names, each featured 12 duplex single rooms and five double bedrooms. The result: space for 22 passengers, all in private rooms. Compare this to 27 passengers in a typical 12-section 1-drawing-room sleeper where most occupants rode in open sections.

HARRY STEGMAIER

the diagram for car 58 that was handed to the Pullman conductor at Philadelphia. The name on the side of this streamlined stainless-steel car has a cheerful ring to it— *Oriole*. It's one of eleven 16-duplex-roomette 4-double-bedroom sleepers built for the B&O in 1954, all named for birds. As the train gets under way, the B&O and Pullman conductors arrive to collect their respective tickets. Accompanying the conductors to compile a passenger list is a B&O train secretary, Ernie Taylor. You know each other from previous trips, and he welcomes you by name. The 33-year veteran of the *Capitol Limited* reminds you that he's on board to provide secretarial services, including taking dictation, typing, and the handling of telegrams sent and received en route.

Soon the porter, a tall, handsome black man of about 50, appears at the door to guide you through the intricacies of the new duplex roomette. These compact, single-person rooms are staggered, split-level style, on either side of a center aisle. Number 8 is on the upper level, reached by a two-step stairway. It features an individual sofa-type seat with armrests, lights for reading and general use, heat and air-conditioning controls, fan, mirror, shoe locker, refrigerated drinking water, fold-away wash basin, and toilet facilities. A pre-made bed folds down from the wall. The porter has stocked the room with towels, bars of soap, and clothes hangers. Here are all the comforts of home, but not much room for luggage! Privacy is ensured

by a sliding door. Lower-level rooms offer the same amenities, but the pre-made bed slides out horizontally from a compartment under the floor of the adjacent upper-level room. Clever!

Noting the fedora you brought along for the spring breezes of Chicago, the porter offers to place it in a Pullman-monogrammed paper hat bag for safe keeping until arrival in the Windy City. He also takes your wake-up call for one-hour before arrival in Chicago; enough time to dress and have breakfast. Finally, he reminds you to place your shoes in the locker if you wish to have them shined during the night. Over the course of the next 15 hours, this man will repeatedly demonstrate an ability, common to most Pullman employees, to give smiling and efficient, yet unobtrusive, service without compromising his dignity. It's not easy, given that some passengers repeatedly hail him with that rather demeaning (and in this case totally inaccurate) cry frequently heard aboard Pullmans: "Hey George!"

The musical sound of chimes passing through the car is immediately recognized as being a waiter from the dining car making the first call for dinner. It's still early, and you want to explore the train before settling down, first, to a cocktail, and then a relaxed meal.

The *Capitol Limited* left Washington tonight with 12 cars and offering only Pullman accommodations. There are no coaches; those desiring overnight coach transportation between Washington and Chicago are aboard the all coach streamliner *Columbian*. From the 120 private rooms in postwar lightweight cars on the *Capitol Limited*, one could have selected a duplex roomette, roomette, single bedroom, double bedroom, two double bedrooms en-suite, or a unique drawing room with two Murphy-style beds. There is also a modernized heavyweight, or "standard" car with 12 open sections of upper and lower berths (accommodations favored by the government for its employees) and a private drawing room.

The lone heavyweight sleeper hearkens back to a time leading into the second decade of the twentieth century when Pullman had successfully standardized accommodations around a single "building block," the open-section, with its two facing chairs by day and upper and lower berths by night. This was by far Pullman's most utilized accommodation at the time as evidenced by its prominence in the company's most popular floor plan: 12 sections and one drawing room, more commonly referred to

as the "12-1." But even as Pullman responded to a growing demand for greater privacy, it did so by simply trying to improve the section through the use of louvered walls in place of curtains along the aisle, or the inclusion of a toilet annex, or—far more successfully—by situating the open section within a larger room. By removing one section, the section on the opposite side of the center aisle could be enclosed in a room that extended nearly across the car some seven feet to a newly created aisle along the now-vacated side of the car. Within this room was a toilet, washbasin, portable chair, and, sometimes, a wardrobe closet.

This design, although found in some Pullman sleeping cars of the late nineteenth century and called a "stateroom," was not fully embraced by Pullman until about 1905. Now marketed as a "compartment," it sold for a price that roughly reflected the fact that it consumed the space of two sections. Meanwhile, the drawing room, a

A postwar product of the Budd Company, Pullman-operated B&O sleeper *Oriole* contained 16 duplex roomettes and 4 double bedrooms. The beds on lower-level rooms were, during the day, rolled away under the floor of the adjacent upper-level room. Eleven of these cars, adorned with bird names, were built for the B&O in 1954 for the Jersey City–Washington–Chicago *Capitol Limited* and the Jersey City–Washington–Louisville/St. Louis *National Limited* and *Diplomat*. Eight of these cars later went to the Seaboard Coast Line and Amtrak where they somtimes served as economy sleepers account of the duplex rooms being slightly smaller than standard roomettes. *HARRY STEGMAIER COLLECTION*

private luxury accommodation that dated from some of the earliest sleeping cars, had already been standardized with a design similar to the new compartment, but with the commode and wash basin located in an enclosed annex, thereby leaving space in the room for a convertible sofa bed along the aisle wall. Because it took up more space than a compartment, the drawing room was priced proportionally higher. Through the use of connecting doors, compartments and drawing rooms could often be used en suite. Pullman "mixed and matched" these three standard designs—sections, compartments, and drawing rooms—to create the various combinations of car accommodations desired by the railroads and traveling public.

A growing concern regarding sleeping cars comprised mainly of sections was the fact that the men's and women's washrooms typically consumed about 25 percent of the useable floor space. The most common floor plan—that of the 12-1 sleeper—had a theoretical capacity of 27 passengers, although one upper berth was generally held for the porter. When filled, the 12-1 was profitable for both Pullman and the railroads. Still, a quarter of the car produced no revenue. However, by the 1920s, the cramped upper berth had fallen into such disfavor with travelers that the saleable capacity of the 12-1 sleeper had effectively dropped to about 18 beds before demand for more lower berth or single occupancy section (SOS) space would prompt the addition of an extra car to a train's consist. Although Pullman could prop up its accommodation revenues from a car by promoting passenger upgrades to SOS or, over time, replacing some or all of the open sections with higher-priced rooms, the railroads were more interested in squeezing additional fare-paying passengers into the car. It was now critically important to both minimize the non-revenue space represented by washrooms and to maximize the number of saleable berths, whether in sections or private rooms.

Happily, the answer—the all-room car—was compatible with the public's growing preference for fully private accommodations. A few all-drawing room and drawing room-compartment cars were built in the next decade for premier luxury trains such as the Santa Fe's *de Luxe*, but these were high-priced rooms with limited appeal for the passenger traveling alone. It appeared that Pullman's drive for standardization and its monopoly position in the sleeping-car business was inhibiting innovation. Nonethe-

less, the railroads pressed on for greater capacity and more marketable accommodations. The single bedroom, introduced in 1927 and priced moderately above an SOS, was a step in the right direction. It featured either a fixed bed or convertible sofa-bed, running transverse to the car, and a portable chair. Since each room contained its own washroom facilities, just a very small public lavatory was needed. However, only 14 rooms could fit into a car, yielding a capacity far short of what the railroads demanded. Soon, the single bedroom evolved into the two-person double bedroom by adding a foldaway upper berth. Goaded by the Pennsylvania Railroad and others, Pullman began in the early 1930s experimenting with "duplex" accommodations that staggered single bedrooms, split-level style, thereby fitting a few more beds into a car.

Changing travel preferences, growing competition, new construction techniques and materials, and creative designers brought about sweeping changes in Pullman's room accommodations between 1937 and 1942. These, and subsequent refinements, raised the effective capacity of the postwar sleeper to as high as 24 people. They are the modern cars you are walking through tonight en route to the *Capitol Limited*'s bar-lounge observation car for a drink.

The most common accommodation on the postwar railroads is the roomette, perfect for a single traveler. It is somewhat larger than your duplex roomette and boasts the same amenities, plus a bit more headroom and luggage space. The bed folds down easily from the wall. Introduced in 1937, the early designs required standing in the aisle behind a protective curtain when lowering or raising the bed and precluded the use of the lavatory facilities when the bed was down. However, the newer cars on the *Capitol Limited* have a cutaway bed that affords some standing room and keeps the wash basin available for use when the bed is down.

The double bedroom has evolved into the second most popular Pullman accommodation and is found in several configurations of seats and berths. The three basic types are available on this train, all offering for one or two passengers the same basic amenities found in your single-person room, plus ample standing room when the beds are down and, in postwar designs, an enclosed annex for the toilet and in, some cases, the wash basin. There are partisans for each of the floor plans. Many passengers favor the traditional transverse convertible sofa and upper berth. Others contend that berths running lengthwise with the car give a better ride and, therefore, choose the version with a short sofa seat and moveable chair. Here, a berth behind the seat folds down longitudinally. The upper berth also generally runs lengthwise. The most recent design affords somewhat greater seating flexibility and room by having two moveable chairs that can be folded and placed under the crosswise-running berths. Some passengers, especially families with children or elderly couples leery of the upper berth, like the fact that the partition between two adjoining double bedrooms can often be opened to provide a large room with four beds or just two lower berths.

Although not offered on the *Capitol Limited*, the mod-ern-day compartment is similar to, but slightly larger than the double bedroom. Designed for two people, it normally has a sofa and moveable chair by day and upper and lower berths by night. In a major improvement over the com-partment of the "standard" era, the toilet and washbasin have been placed in a enclosed annex.

As with its earlier versions, the modern drawing room affords two lower berths and an upper berth at night, but the seating, with a convertible sofa and two moveable chairs, is now more flexible. It continues, of course, to have a private lavatory.

The *Capitol Limited*'s version of the drawing room, found in the Strata-Dome sleeper (featuring a glass-enclosed viewing area upstairs), is unique in that it has three moveable chairs by day, but only two berths that fold out, Murphy-style, from the wall to form twin beds

In addition to the services of a conductor and porter, patrons may have also been served by a Pullman lounge-car attendant, who often worked in Pullman cars comprising both sleeping rooms and public space. Here, patrons are being served in the buffet-lounge section of one of the two 5-double-bedroom buffet-lounge sleepers built in 1950 for assignment to Nickel Plate's new *Nickel Plate Limited* streamliner operating between Chicago, Cleveland, and Buffalo.
THE PULLMAN COMPANY, WILLIAM F. HOWES JR. COLLECTION

at night. This car also offers a modern version of the single bedroom that generally follows the transverse, convertible sofa design of the single bedroom in the "standard" era and the similar duplex single room of today. These one-person accommodations have lavatory facilities within the room that are fully accessible even when the bed in place.

When you reach the observation lounge car, you find it well populated but strangely quiet. Then you realize that the train has just entered West Virginia, a "dry" state. It will be more than an hour before the alcohol flows again, so you order a freshly made orangeade—a Pullman refreshment that became popular during Prohibition—from the attendant and watch the scenery go by. This modern car's decor of light and dark blue fabrics, wood

Arriving rested and refreshed, a Pullman passenger is sent on his way by the Pullman conductor. Often porters would brush off passengers' coats and hats with a small whisk broom upon arrival. Pullman used a new Delaware, Lackawanna & Western 10-6 sleeper as the background for this 1949 publicity photo. THE PULLMAN COMPANY, WILLIAM F. HOWES JR. COLLECTION

veneer, mirrored walls, and fluorescent lighting, although quite attractive, is in marked contrast to the "men's club" atmosphere of the somber and dimly lit *Friars Club* on Pennsy's *Potomac*. After browsing through the car's selection of magazines and today's newspapers, you help yourself to several sheets of monogrammed *Capitol Limited* stationery and an envelope from the writing desk to pen a quick note to a college friend. While in the midst of this, one in a group of three passengers sitting at a table for four waves a two-deck set of Pullman playing cards she's just purchased and suggests you join in a friendly game of Canasta. Just then, a dining-car waiter enters ringing the second call for dinner. You decide to forego the card game in favor of a good meal.

As you enter the diner, steward Claude Murray, another *Capitol* veteran, greets you by name. Although you know it's common on the railroad to seat strangers at the same table, this practice is held to a minimum on All-Pullman runs such as the *Capitol*. Tonight's train has two diners, each offering seating at tables for two or four. The steward seats you alone at a table for two and leaves a check and pencil for you to write out your order. A waiter promptly fills your glass from a bottle of water drawn from B&O's own mountain spring at Deer Park, Maryland.

Everything on the menu looks good, but you know B&O is particularly noted for its Chesapeake Bay seafood. Tonight it's Boned Bay Shad with Roe. You decide to start with a cup of consomme and vermicelli, and, of course, you'll end the meal with a slice of warm apple pie with cheddar cheese. A waiter retrieves and repeats your written order and delivers it to the kitchen. Shortly, he's back at your table with a huge bowl of salad topped with Catalina dressing and crumbled blue cheese, from which he invites you to "help yourself" in filling your salad plate.

Surveying your fellow passengers in the diner, you see a few military uniforms in a sea of brown, blue, black, and gray business suits. Except for two attractively dressed women sitting next to you, it's an all male crowd!

The meal is everything you had hoped it would be. Satisfied, you head for the Strata-Dome car, just in time for a moonlit assault on the Allegheny Mountains. Then, on your way back to your sleeper, you remember you have yet to make a hotel reservation for your overnight stay in Chicago. Fortunately, there's a copy of the Hotel

Red Book and Western Union telegraph blanks in each car. Deciding on the Palmer House, you compose a telegram requesting a room, and go in search of the Train Secretary. As suspected, he's in the club car at the head end of the train, typing letters. He takes your telegram and promises to hand it to the agent at Pittsburgh to send. Lingering in the lounge for a few minutes to listen to the radio, you quickly conclude that this is truly a "male preserve." A dozen men sit with drinks by their side, puffing on cigars, pipes or cigarettes—some conversing, others reading—all to the muffled sounds of the diesel locomotives working up ahead. Your memory flashes back 15 years or so, to your first trip on the *Capitol Limited*, when you sat here listening to the rhythmic blasts of a steam engine helping the diesels conquer these hills. It was also a time when the services of a barber and valet were available in this car, while elsewhere a maid-manicurist tended to the needs of women and children on the train.

It's time to retire for the night. Since the bed in your room is already made up and merely needs to be pulled out from the wall, you complete the task without the help of the porter. The bed fills the room, presenting a challenge nearly as daunting as preparing for bed in a lower berth. When first introduced by Pullman in 1942, the duplex roomette was thought to be the logical replacement for the open-section berth. Although ultimately eclipsed by the popularity of the more spacious roomette, it was, indeed, an improvement. But preparing for bed still calls for a good bit of agility. B&O isn't the smoothest riding railroad on the map, but sleep comes easily. Perhaps it's the fact that duplex roomette 8 is toward the center of the car, where the ride is always smoother.

The next thing you hear is the buzzer by your door and the porter advising that the train is now one hour from Chicago. For a 50-cent service fee, you can have breakfast brought to your room. But there is something special about the smell of a dining car in the morning that prompts you to shave, dress, and head for a "Good Morning" demitasse, compliments of the B&O, and a breakfast of sugar-cured bacon, scrambled eggs, and toast topped with apple butter.

Once back in your room, the porter arrives to pick up your bags and inquire if you will need a Red Cap. He also

offers to brush off your clothes, a service which dates back to the days of steam locomotives and before air-conditioning. You follow the advice of the newspaper's etiquette columnist who says, "Tip the Pullman Porter $1 per person per night."

At 8:30 a.m., the *Capitol Limited* arrives in Grand Central Station, Chicago; not early, not late, simply on time. You look forward to your return trip east tomorrow in Pullman safety and comfort.

Pullman's classy travel posters of the 1930s incorporated the company's slogan, ". . . in Pullman Safety & Comfort." *JOE WELSH COLLECTION*

RIGHT: Photographed from 18th Street, Pennsylvania Railroad's all-Pullman *Broadway Limited* makes its grand departure from Chicago for Philadelphia and New York on a late-summer's afternoon in 1960. Sixteen hours of pampering at the hands of Pullman and railroad staff lay ahead for *Broadway* patrons. The *Broadway* would earn the distinction of being one of the last all-Pullman operations in the U.S., vying with Illinois Central's *Panama Limited* and Chesapeake & Ohio's seasonal *Resort Special*. The honor of being the very last scheduled all-Pullman train in the U.S. would finally go to the *Resort Special* operating bi-weekly between Washington, D.C., and the Homestead and Greenbrier resorts at Hot Springs, Virginia, and White Sulphur Springs, West Virginia, respectively. The *Special* made its final run November 10, 1968. JOHN DZIOBKO

INSET: The PRR continued to promote its *Broadway Limited* almost to the end of the Pennsylvania Railroad itself in 1968. Dating from 1960, this brochure featured the train's Pullman staff. JOE WELSH COLLECTION

New challenges arose for The Pullman Company at the end of World War II. Court-mandated reorganization raised questions about the company's future while mounting competition from the automobile and the airlines threatened to steal its customers. But Pullman survived the challenges of reorganization. As a partner with the railroads and carrying over 31 million passengers in 1945, Pullman was too important a service to discontinue or carve up.

Ultimately, though, the speed of the airplane and the convenience of the auto would defeat the railroads—and Pullman would be one of the harbingers of the problem. By the beginning of the 1950s, Pullman's first-class business passengers had begun forsaking its comfortable overnight sleepers for a quick airplane ride. Meanwhile, families that Pullman hoped to carry on vacation chose instead to wander Eisenhower's new "Defense Highway System"—the Interstate—in their new car, eating at Howard Johnson's, staying at a Holiday Inn, and paying 28 cents a gallon for gas.

ABOVE: The top "name" trains may have gotten the glory and the advertising but Pullman really earned its stripes providing convenient, comfortable service on hundreds of secondary trains. In this sequence taken in 1946, Central Vermont's southbound *Vermonter* is pictured as it pauses behind 4-8-2 No. 600 under an ancient wooden train shed at Essex Junction, Vermont. RIGHT: Sandwiched between a wooden milk car and a heavyweight coach, 12-section 1-drawing-room Pullman *Cosmopolitan* provides the *Vermonter*'s sole sleeping-car accommodations. It's covering a line from St. Albans, Vermont, to Pennsylvania Station in New York City. The car will be carried as far south as White River Junction, Vermont, on the *Vermonter* where it will transfer to the southbound *Washingtonian* for the remainder of the journey. Although Pullman received over 1,600 new lightweight sleeping cars after World War II, two thirds of its service was still provided by heavyweights like this into the early 1950s. BOTH PHOTOS, PHILLIP R. HASTINGS, M.D. COLLECTION, CALIFORNIA STATE RAILROAD MUSEUM, JOE WELSH COLLECTION

In response to this growing challenge, the railroads and Pullman introduced beautiful, innovative, and new post-war trains. Dome cars, streamlined equipment, and faster schedules combined with old-fashioned, comfortable service made American trains the best in the world as the 1950s dawned. These new trains and cars shared the rails with older stalwarts that were running out their last miles in service. It was unquestionably the best time in history to ride an American passenger train, and it lasted for only a little over two decades. In 1945 Pullman operated over 5,500 cars; by 1968 it ran just 425. By the middle of 1969, Pullman would exit the passenger transport business after 102 years of service.

The legacy of Pullman's service remains a fond memory for those who have ridden its cars. For those who never had the chance, the history of what Pullman provided in the 1950s and 1960s marked the last, best effort of a great American company to provide a transportation service where "First Class" meant more than just an extra inch of seat width on the five-hour flight to somewhere.

REORGANIZATION AND NEW OWNERSHIP

As the result of the 1944 final judgement of the Federal District Court in the anti-trust case of 1940, Pullman Incorporated was forced to separate its operating arm, The Pullman Company, from its manufacturing arm, the Pullman-Standard Car Manufacturing Company. In May 1945 Pullman Incorporated offered to sell the capital stock of The Pullman Company at a price based upon the depreciated value of its cars, facilities, and other physical assets to a consortium of railroads. There followed a complex transaction that would eventually be valued at over $75 million.

Due to the 1944 court action, Pullman also notified the railroads that, effective December 31, 1945, its operating contracts with them would be terminated. In 1945, Pullman had carried over 31 million passengers in

An interesting operating practice of The Pullman Company was the "set-out" sleeper—cars that were set out and picked up at towns along the route of through trains so that local passengers could board and alight at a more civilized hour. The practice extended into the postwar period but due to costs was virtually eliminated by 1960. In this intriguing photo taken in 1946 at Burlington, Vermont, a Rutland Railroad switcher has coupled up to a heavyweight sleeper serving as the Burlington set-out car; the car has already taken on its passengers, most of whom are probably asleep. The switcher will couple the car to the New York-bound *Mount Royal* out of Montreal once it arrives in Burlington. *PHILLIP R. HASTINGS, M.D. COLLECTION, CALIFORNIA STATE RAILROAD MUSEUM, JOE WELSH COLLECTION*

its 5,500 cars as a result of the war. In other words, it was an enormous and invaluable American transportation enterprise—one that could not easily be replaced by the railroads who depended on Pullman to carry sleeping-car passengers on their own trains in a cost-effective manner. In October 1945, 20 railroads, which handled over 80 percent of the sleeping-car business in the U.S., signed a memorandum of agreement to maintain without interruption the vital service Pullman provided while endeavoring to sell the company to another concern by December 31, 1948.

Shortly thereafter, the railroads changed their mind about the sale of Pullman and wanted to buy it, but not before other parties also took an interest in purchasing the company. Of these, the biggest threat to the railroads was flamboyant financier Robert R. Young (a "takeover artist" in today's parlance) who enraged the entrenched railroad industry by pointing out its passenger-service flaws—and there were plenty—in the national press.

Concerned about Young owning a service they would all depend on, in November 1945 a "Buying Group" of railroads officially offered to purchase the stock of The Pullman Company. In December 1945 the lower Court gave its blessing to the sale, but not until March 1947 did a divided U.S. Supreme Court hand down a final opinion supporting the sale to the Buying Group of railroads.

On June 30, 1947, Pullman Inc. and a buying group of 57 (later, 59) railroads consummated the agreement. Pullman Inc. received over $40 million for the Pullman operating company. The owning railroads subscribed for Pullman stock shares in the ratio of sleeping cars operated on their line to the total number of sleeping cars operated in 1940.

The equipment transactions were equally Byzantine. Pullman had previously owned almost all the cars it operated, but as a result of the 1944 court action, it was ordered to sell much of its equipment. In December 1945, Pullman sold 601 lightweight sleeping cars and 256

With its sofa seat by day, single bed at night, complete lavatory facilities, and individually controlled lighting and temperature, the roomette provided the comfort and privacy long sought by passengers traveling alone. More roomettes were included in the sleeping-car fleet built after World War II than any other accommodation. They were particularly popular with people on business trips. A portable table facilitated doing work en route. When the bed was lowered, the seat in which this traveler is sitting automatically folded down under the bed; the foot end of the bed covered the toilet. Thus, not only did roomettes have wall-to-wall carpeting, they had wall-to-wall beds. *THE PULLMAN COMPANY, WILLIAM F. HOWES JR. COLLECTION*

(mostly heavyweight) parlor cars to the railroads at a cost of over $35 million; then they were leased back to Pullman for operation. Pullman also issued "Car Notes"—essentially dividends to its owner railroads that reduced the railroads' investment in Pullman stock from $40 million to $27 million, and the railroads took ownership of an additional 2,444 heavyweight Pullman cars. Remaining in Pullman ownership were 2,875 heavyweight cars and 6 lightweight cars, forming the backbone of the Pullman Pool—a flexible source of capacity that could be used to cover seasonal fluctuations in demand, unexpected troop movements, and charter group moves. New cars built for Pullman use would have to be purchased by the railroads directly from the car builders.

THE "NEW" PULLMAN COMPANY

The new Pullman operating company looked a lot like the old company. Virtually no operating changes occurred

Continued on page 114

BELOW: A typical "crosswise" bedroom accommodation, in "day" mode, in a postwar, lightweight sleeping car. In a crosswise bedroom, the three-seat sofa at right folded down into a lower bed while the upper bed folded out of the ceiling above. In a "lengthwise" bedroom, both upper and lower beds were parallel to the rails. *ROBERT P. SCHMIDT*

The "standard" Pullman lightweight sleeping car of the postwar period was the 10-roomette 6-double-bedroom car, better known as the "10 & 6" or simply "10-6." Hundreds of the type with different floor plans and flashy exterior finishes operated on numerous railroads from coast to coast. The Delaware, Lackawanna & Western Railroad, a regional carrier linking Buffalo and Hoboken, received nine 10-6 sleeping cars from builder American Car & Foundry and leased them to Pullman for operation in 1949; shown is the *Tioughnioga*. In keeping with typical Pullman practice, the cars were named rather than numbered. Lackawanna's cars were named for local landmarks and carried tongue-twisting Indian names. Pronounced "Tie-UFF-nee-OH-ga," Tioughnioga means "meeting of waters" and was the name of a small river which empties into the Chenango River. *ACF INDUSTRIES, JOE WELSH COLLECTION*

Keeping the Fleet Running

For most Pullman travelers, the human face of the company was projected by the smiling Pullman conductor collecting tickets at the beginning of a trip, or the porter anticipating one's needs en route, or the efficient attendant in the Pullman-operated buffet-lounge car. At the peak of its peacetime business in the late 1920s, Pullman's on-board service personnel numbered nearly 13,000.

And yet, for every employee out on the trains, there was the equivalent of another 1.25 employees working behind the scenes to keep the fleet running and the service standards high. In fact, fully 40 percent of Pullman's workforce was devoted to the cleaning, maintenance, or repair of its thousands of "rolling hotels."

Pullman, of course, had people engaged in finance, accounting, legal, labor relations, personnel, and public relations activities at its Chicago headquarters. And, there was a traffic department to establish rates for Pullman's accommodations, publish and file tariffs with regulatory agencies, distribute ticket stock, and process passenger refunds. It also promoted Pullman travel, although it did so generically to avoid the appearance of favoring one railroad over another.

But the real focal point of The Pullman Company was its operating department. Here rested responsibility for the movement, staffing, supplying, cleaning, servicing, maintenance, repair, and engineering of cars through an organization of system and railroad terminal offices, as well as shops, storehouses, laundries and commissaries.

The underlying strength of George Pullman's business plan was that it (1) offered the traveler consistent, high-quality standards of service and equipment maintenance nationwide without regard to the specific railroad(s) over which a car was operating; and (2) it provided a pool of equipment and staff to meet special needs and seasonal variations in demand. The car service function within the operating department sought to maximize the utilization of each car in revenue service and hold to a minimum out-of-service time and deadhead movements. Car distributors maintained current records of available cars, their type of accommodations, and other physical characteristics. Much of this equipment was assigned to regular sleeping- or parlor-car lines. The remainder formed a pool from which to handle emergency movements or fill seasonal and other special requests. This could be particularly challenging when such requests involved a large number of cars. One such event, the annual Kentucky Derby, generally required assembling several hundred sleepers from the pool to operate in regular and special trains from various origins to Louisville and return.

In its heyday, Pullman's cars were serviced in upwards of 300 railroad yards. There were district offices at terminals that originated a large number of car lines while agency offices were maintained at less active cities. As of 1930, Pullman had a total of 86 district and agency offices throughout North America. They played a key role in the distribution of cars by setting up movements through their car desk clerk's daily reporting of equipment in service or standing at that location. In the days of telegraph communications, this huge volume of messages became manageable through the use of a cipher code. For example, the code word "Dog" followed by the name of the car was all that was needed to transmit the message: "Car [name] is here. Advise disposition."

The districts and agencies were also responsible for providing conductors, porters, attendants and bus boys for car originations in their territory. Typically, car service employees would go on duty at the crew sign-out office several hours before the train's departure. Conductors used the time to check the condition of the Pullmans in the train's consist, assemble trip documents and review them with the porters, and greet passengers. Porters made sure their car was prepared for occupancy and assisted boarding passengers. Attendants and bus boys obtained keys to their restaurant, buffet, or lounge car from the commissary, stored supplies, and readied the car for service. At the completion of their runs, the employees remitted their revenue and ticket collections to the receiving cashier for forwarding to the Accounting Department.

LEFT: Pullman painters were veritable artists at finishing cars. This worker is masking the striping on a *20th Century Limited* sleeper-lounge observation car in 1938. *LARRY TYE*

ABOVE: Periodic maintenance and repainting of Pullman cars, as well as heavy repairs and remodeling, was performed at company shops strategically placed around the U.S. *THE PULLMAN COMPANY, WILLIAM F. HOWES JR. COLLECTION*

BELOW: This transfer table was used to move Pullmans between the bays of its shop. *THE PULLMAN COMPANY, WILLIAM F. HOWES JR. COLLECTION*

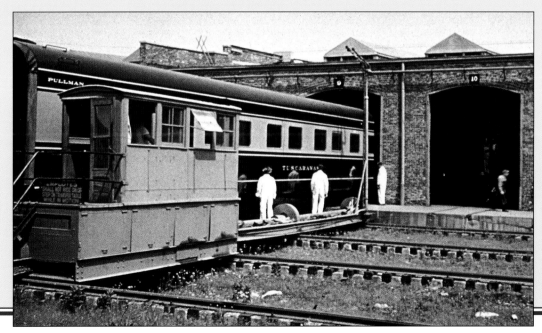

Mechanical and service problems noted en route were recorded by each car's porter, verified by Pullman's conductor, and reported to the yard foreman at destination for correction.
THE PULLMAN COMPANY, WILLIAM F. HOWES JR. COLLECTION

Car service employees not assigned to regular lines were available for extra or special service. They could also be temporarily assigned to other districts to meet seasonal demands. Some major locations also employed uniformed platform agents to assist Pullman passengers before or after their trip and to handle emergency situations. Traveling service supervisors and porter instructors ensured that Pullman's standards of service were being maintained.

District and agency offices generally had a shop and storeroom staffed to clean, supply, and perform running maintenance on Pullmans. The company's commitment to the interior cleanliness of its equipment is reflected in the fact that roughly one out of eight Pullman employees was engaged in car cleaning. In addition to car cleaners, the yard foreman would typically have a staff of carmen, electricians, upholsterers, and painters, while the storekeeper had car suppliers, linen checkers, linen carriers, and clerks. Each Pullman arriving at a terminal was accompanied by an inspection report on which car service employees and inspectors recorded defects or other problems. This information, plus any periodic maintenance required, defined the day's work for the yard. Among the periodic tasks were flushing water tanks every 30 days, shampooing carpets every 60 days, and cleaning, inspecting, and lubricating air-conditioning equipment weekly.

Many districts also had commissaries that were responsible for handling supplies and equipment in support of Pullman's food and beverage services aboard restau-rant, buffet, and lounge cars that at one time operated on some 400 car lines. Sometimes likened to a chain of super-markets, Pullman maintained a central commissary at Chicago, major commissaries at New York City (Pennsylvania's Sunnyside Yard and New York Central's Mott Haven Yard), St. Louis, and Washington, D.C., and smaller facilities at nearly two-dozen other locations, including four yards in Chicago. A number of yard storerooms also handled commissary supplies. Commissary employment varied greatly over time, reaching nearly 500 in 1940, peaking well over 700 during World War II, and then steadily declining as restaurant, parlor-buffet, and lounge-car services were curtailed.

Typically, commissary checkers would board cars arriving in the terminal yard to inventory foodstuffs and equipment, prepare a transfer report of any items being removed, advise the commissary of restocking requirements, and secure the car. Commissary clerks stripped and restocked cars and handled supplies within the commissary. Traveling inspectors periodically reviewed commissary activities, including sanitary practices. Pullman took pride in its cuisine and methodically trained its chefs, attendants, and bus boys in its proper preparation and serving upon the Company's distinctive "Indian Tree" pattern china. Passengers were particularly fond of the double lamb chops and imported Portuguese sardines. By 1960, the service had been largely reduced to just beverages and light meals such as a chilled salmon plate.

Graphically descriptive job titles such as body builder, stripper, painter, cabinet-maker, pipe-fitter, glazier, carpet-cutter, seamstress, and feather-renovator hint of the scope and diversity of the work performed by Pullman's six shops for major equipment repairs and renovations. Located at Calumet (Chicago), St. Louis, Buffalo, Wilmington, Del., Richmond, Calif., and Atlanta, each shop was remarkably self-sufficient. Functional named departments included Body-Joiner-Trim, Cabinet, Iron, Welding, Tin & Brass, Glass & Mirror, Upholstery & Carpet, Pillow, Electric, Steam, Platform & Truck, Air Brake and Paint.

Cars were generally shopped at 30- to 36-month intervals. They were stripped of parts to be tested, repaired, renovated, or replaced. Programmed work typically included replacement of window gaskets; truck, brake, and air-conditioning overhaul; upholstery, carpet, and bedding renovation or replacement; plating of hardware; and painting. The shops also repaired and renovated parts for use by the district yards. The office of chief engineer developed the engineering designs for any remodeling of cars, as well as specifications for products and equipment used by the shops. This office also maintained a test department for evaluating compliance with Pullman's rigorous standards.

Supporting the six heavy-repair shops were storerooms that were part of a systemwide department devoted to ordering and stocking supplies and parts for car cleaning, maintenance, and repair. With a general storeroom at

Calumet Shops, the Purchases & Stores department operated more than 200 satellite storerooms at railroad yards servicing Pullman cars. Drawing from a standard catalog of some 75,000 items, the department might have on hand at any time nearly 10,000 different items for distribution. The late 1920s saw a linen inventory of more than 7 million towels and sheets, with annual replenishment purchases of over a million towels and nearly 400,000 sheets.

P&S also operated 10 laundries strategically located around the country, and it also contracted with railroad and commercial laundries at numerous locations. Employment at Pullman laundries grew to 554 in 1940 with positions such as washerman, mangle worker, seamstress, and linen servicer. World War II saw employment approach 1,000 and production reach 2.6 million sheets and pillowcases and 1.5 million towels per week. By 1950, employment had dropped again to 562 and con-

tinued to decline as laundries closed until only two facilities remained in 1966.

Although most of Pullman's activities directly tracked the decline in its passenger traffic through the 1960s, its car service and maintenance functions held on somewhat longer than the staffing of cars. For example, when the Pennsylvania Railroad entered into a "partial form of service" contract with Pullman on its local lines in August 1967, Pullman continued to lease and maintain Pennsylva-

nia's sleepers while the railroad provided porters and collected ticket revenue. Other railroads followed suit, and Pullman ceased staffing any cars in the U.S. or Canada effective January 1, 1969. Although this date has often been bannered as the end of The Pullman Company, it continued to lease and maintain a fleet of sleepers for assigned and pool service until the railroads took over these functions on August 1, 1969. Pullman's Mexican operations continued until late 1970.

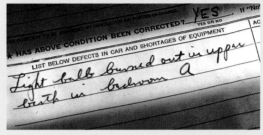

Upon each car's arrival at its destination, yard forces went to work cleaning (LEFT), correcting (ABOVE), and making repairs (RIGHT) prepatory to the car's next trip. Some trains and their Pullman cars laid over for only a few hours at destinations, requiring Pullman personnel to perform work as promptly as possible to ensure on-time departures.

BELOW: Pullman's launderies processed millions of sheets, pillow cases, towels, antimacassars (headrests), and table linens each week. *ALL PHOTOS, THIS PAGE, THE PULLMAN COMPANY, WILLIAM F. HOWES JR. COLLECTION*

Continued from page 109

at Pullman, which for decades had been a well-oiled machine. The national company still divided the country into zones (by 1951 they were called "regions") with a regional manager in charge of a number of districts. These were parceled into smaller agencies located at the terminals of most of the passenger-carrying railroads in the United States and at some places in Canada and Mexico. The districts were run by a superintendent and the agencies by an agent. Most passenger terminal yards had a Pullman store room and mechanical shop in the charge of a storekeeper and a foreman, with car cleaners and mechanics also on staff. At the larger yards, a Pullman commissary continued to provide dining-service support. Specialists were assigned to support the regional managers, and the Pullman headquarters staff in Chicago also provided operating assistance. All of these, including the chief mechanical officer, came under the watchful eye of the vice president of operations. The chief mechanical officer oversaw the engineering department, the test department and laboratory (at one time Pullman tested everything

ABOVE: Behind the scenes, hundreds of clerical employees processed—without the aid of computers— the tickets, diagrams, work reports, and myriad other documents generated daily by one of the nation's largest and most far-flung enterprises. *THE PULLMAN COMPANY, WILLIAM F. HOWES JR. COLLECTION*

RIGHT: The Pullman yard storekeeper's linen carrier transports bags of clean laundery to waiting sleepers at Santa Fe's 18th Street Coach Yard in Chicago ca. 1950. *THE PULLMAN COMPANY, WILLIAM F. HOWES JR. COLLECTION*

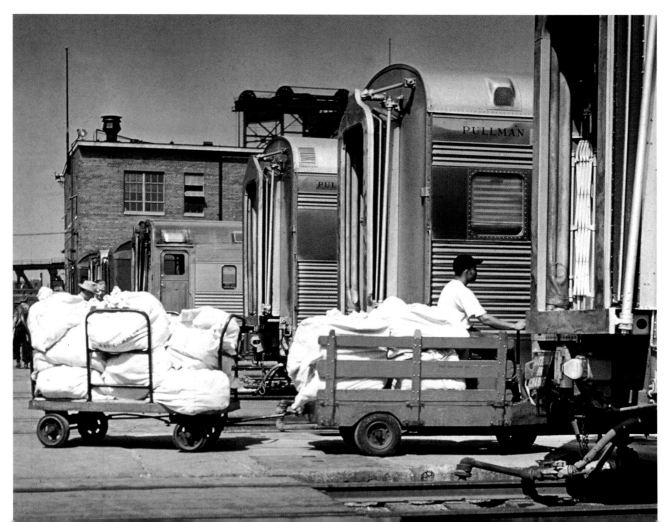

from the steel it used in its cars to the feathers with which it stuffed pillows), six major repair shops and ten laundries spread across the country.

Existing before the computer age, Pullman's tracking of supply and demand was a complex ballet of paperwork, Teletype, and telephone. Moving thousands of cars and employees around nightly was not a task for the faint of heart, but Pullman excelled at it. Whether it was extra linens needed in San Antonio (Pullman once required over 7 million pieces of linen to conduct its daily operations) or a fleet of cars required to handle a convention group headed for Chicago, Pullman met the challenge with aplomb. Its transportation department (renamed Car Service in 1951) operated its cars on Pullman "lines" connecting geographical endpoints, and these lines were tracked closely. The company received daily reports from all over North America showing cars used in regular and extra (pool) service and the number of cars left at each endpoint each night. Pullman also tracked orders for future travel, such as the seasonal rush to Florida in winter

The linen locker space aboard each sleeping, parlor, or buffet car was designed to accommodate the requirements of that car for a typical trip. *THE PULLMAN COMPANY, WILLIAM F. HOWES JR. COLLECTION*

Pullman prided itself on the ride quality of its cars. This required periodic inspection and maintenance of each car's wheel assemblies, or "trucks." *THE PULLMAN COMPANY, WILLIAM F. HOWES JR. COLLECTION*

TOP: Delivered in 1950, *Ashley River* was a Pullman car with a rare floor plan, 14 roomettes and 2 drawing rooms. Built by Pullman Standard's competitor American Car & Foundry, it carries the distinctive purple letterboards of the Atlantic Coast Line Railroad. ACL was one of Pullman's best customers, operating sold-out trains to Florida from the Midwest and along the Eastern seaboard for years. *ACF INDUSTRIES, JOE WELSH COLLECTION*

TOP: Pullman car Oleander built in 1950 was a 6-double-bedroom 24-seat buffet-lounge car. Finished in Florida East Coast Railroad's stainless-steel colors to match its primarily Budd-built fleet, the car typically operated between New York and Florida. *ACF INDUSTRIES, JOE WELSH COLLECTION*

or the annual Kentucky Derby and marshaled cars to meet the demand.

Pullman first-class sleeping and parlor cars operated in the same trains as the cars of the railroads that contracted with Pullman, which typically provided their own dining cars and coaches on the same run. Pullman provided this service for its owner railroad under the terms of the Uniform Service Contract of 1949. The contract established that Pullman would furnish cars as required by the railroad, which in turn sold Pullman tickets along with its own. Pullman was responsible for maintaining, cleaning, supplying, and staffing the cars; the railroad handled the exterior cleaning and running-gear inspection and lubrication. Exterior repairs, such as to trucks, performed by

the railroad would be billed to Pullman. If Pullman performed work for which the railroad was contractually responsible, it would bill the railroad.

When revenues exceeded expenses on a particular Pullman service, the railroad kept 75 percent of the profit and Pullman got the remainder. When expenses exceeded revenues, the railroad was required to make up the deficit to Pullman. This latter fact, coupled with the fact that the railroads owned Pullman, explains why Pullman service shrunk so fast when profits dried up in the 1950s.

A NEW STREAMLINED PULLMAN ERA

All of this service was being provided by a rapidly changing fleet of cars and trains in response to competition

ABOVE: Finished with light green or tan walls and featuring cedar-colored Pullman blankets, *Ashley River*'s drawing room reflects the typical lightweight Pullman room of the 1950s and 1960s. *ACF INDUSTRIES, JOE WELSH COLLECTION*

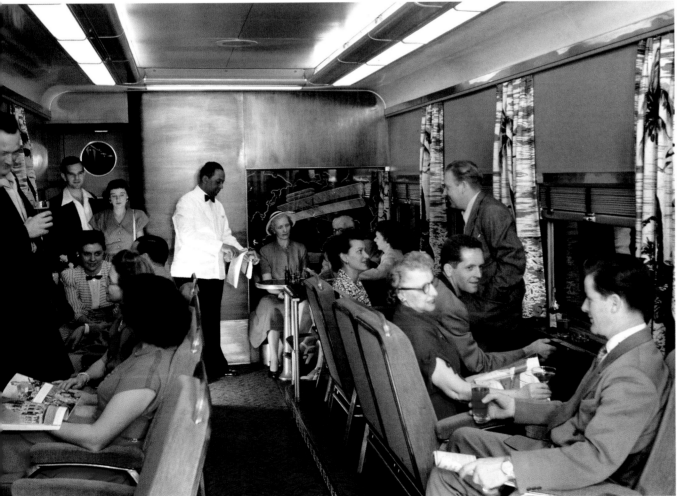

LEFT: *Oleander* and the other eight cars in the order—six cars for ACL, two total for FEC (*Magnolia* was *Oleander*'s sister car), and one for Richmond, Fredericksburg & Potomac— featured interiors with a 24-seat lounge for first-class passengers. The seats, which sat on a raised floor level, faced outward for viewing. *ACF INDUSTRIES, JOE WELSH COLLECTION*

ABOVE: The Pullman parlor car, featuring a single swiveling chair and the attention of a Pullman porter, was shrinking in popularity by the early 1950s. A long time stronghold of parlor-car service was the Pennsylvania Railroad, and in 1952, the PRR re-equipped its premier New York–Washington, D.C., daytime trains, the *Congressionals* and the *Senator* (Boston–Washington) with lightweight cars. Here, parlor-observation car *George Washington* brings up the rear of the eastbound *Morning Congressional* at Trenton, New Jersey, in August 1953. *JOHN DZIOBKO JOE WELSH COLLECTION*

RIGHT: Businessmen seem to dominate the Pullman check-in counters at Chicago Union Station circa 1953 for PRR's *Gotham Limited*, *Southland*, and *Daytonian*, and Burlington's *Western Star* and *Ak-Sar-Ben Zephyr*, providing overnight, early morning arrival service to Pittsburgh, Cincinnati, Dayton, St. Paul/Minneapolis, and Omaha, respectively. *THE PULLMAN COMPANY, WILLIAM F. HOWES JR. COLLECTION*

and use. The travel impacts of World War II, when demand had quadrupled, had worn out older equipment and prematurely aged newer prewar streamlined equipment. The competition was increasing more than ever. Between 1946 and 1954 America spent $20 billion on highway construction. The effort would go into high gear with the 1956 enactment of federal legislation to create a 40,000-mile Defense Highway System, better known as the Interstate. Between the end of the war and the advent of the Interstate, Americans had already bought 37 million autos.

The airline industry was also a growing threat. In 1950, Pullman and the domestic airlines each handled about 16 million passengers annually. Pullman's business dropped to 13 million passengers by 1953; the same year, airlines carried 26 million passengers. With the advent of domestic jet airline service in 1958, the competition became incredibly stiff, overwhelming Pullman. But in the decade after World War II, between 1946 and 1956, before the contest was decided, American railroads had re-equipped their passenger trains at an amazing rate. Over 4,400 lightweight railroad passenger cars were constructed, of which 1,603 were sleeping cars for lease to Pullman. The industry spent over $1.3 billion on new equipment during this period.

POSTWAR PULLMAN CARS

The new cars were made of lightweight metals, streamlined in appearance, finished in attractive colors or stainless steel, and beautifully appointed inside. The cars also came in a staggering variety of designs. In fact, so many new styles had emerged that Pullman, which had always depended on standardization to keep its national operating costs under control, found itself complaining to the car-buying railroads. Pullman complained about floor plans that confused ticket agents and mechanical systems that, while easily maintained on the owning road, baffled servicing personnel when operating off-line. To address the issue, Pullman and the railroads made a new attempt at standardization, introducing cars, designed by committees, that were more intelligently planned than their brethren cranked out in the early heat of postwar optimism. Examples included cars built for the Chesapeake & Ohio, New York, Chicago & St. Louis (Nickel Plate), Pere Marquette, and Louisville & Nashville.

All of these new cars rejuvenated a service suffering from a reputation as being old and outdated. Although almost all the types of rooms introduced in postwar sleeping cars were based on those introduced immediately before the war or earlier, there were bright new colors and intelligent upgrades. Improving on its prewar version, the Pullman bedroom, for example, received enclosed lavatory facilities—a necessary improvement in a room that seated two passengers.

The classic Pullman open section in which two patrons (often total strangers) sat facing each other all day and slept in berths one above the other separated only by heavy green curtains had once been Pullman's standard accommodation. But the section had been declining in popularity since the late 1920s because patrons wanted more privacy and no longer wanted to ride in claustrophobic upper berths. In the 1930s, for example, the Pennsylvania Railroad observed that while it could fill 77 percent of its lower berths, only 18 percent of the uppers were being occupied.

The Pullman open section was shrinking in popularity by the 1930s, but the accommodation survived into the post-World War II era by many years, though not on many trains. Here a mother and daughter converse with the Pullman conductor in the open section of a heavyweight car that's been modernized for post-World War II use. *THE PULLMAN COMPANY, WILLIAM F. HOWES JR. COLLECTION*

ABOVE: At the Pullman plant in Chicago, workers mask, for painting, the solarium end of one member of a fleet of the most unusual streamlined Pullman cars ever built, the Skytop sleeper. The Milwaukee Road had six of these 8-bedroom lounge-observation cars built in 1949 for its Chicago–Tacoma, Wash., *Olympian Hiawatha*. THE PULLMAN COMPANY, WILLIAM F. HOWES JR. COLLECTION

RIGHT: Sporting its new Skytop sleeper-lounge observation car as well as one of the new 10-6 sleepers the Milwaukee purchased in 1949, the westbound *Olympian Hiawatha* speeds its way through Montana's "Big Sky" country. THE MILWAUKEE ROAD, MILWAUKEE ROAD HISTORICAL ASSOCIATION ARCHIVES

Although the number of new cars featuring sections declined during the postwar period, some railroads continued to show loyalty to the accommodation, incorporating it in new floor plans with a mix of sections, bedrooms, and roomettes. It was well known that the government only paid the section rate for employees traveling on the government payroll and the railroads didn't want to design themselves out of a market by eliminating the section entirely. Even in peacetime, up to 12 percent of Pullman's business came from the government. Ironically, however, the railroads also had some all-section cars built after the war. They were targeted at budget-minded tourists traveling primarily in the West—a solid market for the company in prewar years. Postwar, Pullman operated new all-section cars briefly on three of the most famous streamliners in the west: the new *California Zephyr* introduced in 1949 as well as on the re-equipped *City of Portland* and *Challenger* of 1954.

In direct response to changing customer needs, the fully enclosed roomette, first introduced in 1937, replaced the section as the most desirable accommodation to individual travelers in postwar travel. It was incorporated in hundreds of new Pullman cars, either by itself or in mixed configurations with other types of sleeping accommodations, usually double bedrooms. The roomette was a miracle of efficiency, sleeping one passenger and incorporating a bed, a sink, a toilet, a closet and a big picture window, all in a space hardly bigger than a broom closet.

Prior to streamlining, the 12-section 1-drawing-room (12-1) car had been the standard-bearer in Pullman's fleet. After the war, that mantle would eventually fall to the streamlined "10-6" or "10-and-6" with 10 roomettes and 6 double bedrooms. The cars could be found operating in every nook and cranny of the U.S. New York Central, for

example, ordered 97 *River*-series 10-6s from Pullman-Standard and another 40 in the *Valley* series from car builder Budd Company. That group alone amounted to almost one tenth of the total number of streamlined Pullmans delivered after World War II.

Pullman was also operating more exotic floor plans and car types. Among the most unusual were dome sleepers (B&O, NP, CB&Q, SP&S, UP) and dome sleeper-observation cars (CB&Q, D&RGW, and WP) that offered rooftop viewing for first-class patrons. Pullman service in domed parlor cars was also available on the Wabash Railroad.

Parlor cars, which featured first-class daytime accommodations, usually plush rotating chairs, never comprised more than about three percent of the total number of passenger cars operating nationwide. Except for a few cars built for some Midwestern and Western roads, most of

MAIN PHOTO: Pullman observation car *La Mirada* was owned by Rock Island and built for the Golden Rocket, a proposed-but-never-implemented Chicago–Los Angeles service joint with Southern Pacific. Pictured on display at the Chicago Railroad Fair of 1948–49, the car later was assigned to the newly streamlined Golden State between Chicago and Los Angeles. *GEORGE KRAMBLES, KRAMBLES-PETERSON ARCHIVE*

INSET: The forward bulkhead wall of *La Mirada's* swank lounge section mimicked the curved lines of the observation area. *PULLMAN-STANDARD, WILLIAM F. HOWES JR. COLLECTION*

which provided their own parlor service, lightweight parlor cars were largely confined to Eastern roads such as the New Haven and the Pennsylvania during postwar years. New Haven replaced most of its heavyweight parlor car fleet with dozens of streamlined lightweight cars in the late 1940s, but the frugal Pennsy chose to replace only the parlors operating on its top day trains, the *Congressionals* and the *Senator*, in 1952. Both roads used Pullman to operate their parlor service until 1956.

Ironically, the introduction of all these nice, new lightweight cars rendered their heavyweight brethren obsolete almost overnight in the minds of travelers—a big problem for Pullman because the heavyweights still comprised a majority of its fleet into the early 1950s. In 1951, two thirds of Pullman's daily departures occurred in heavyweight cars. As demand declined and heavyweight cars could be rapidly retired, by 1956 only one third of Pullman departures occurred in heavyweight cars.

These new streamlined Pullmans and many repainted heavyweight Pullmans came in a rainbow of paint schemes and finishes, reflecting the trend of the day as their owning railroads now sought to distinguish their trains with bright new liveries or shining stainless steel. Fading were the days of the ubiquitous, Pullman green sleeping car.

POSTWAR PULLMAN TRAIN SERVICE

The trains on which these cars operated ranged from household names to obscure runs identified only by their train numbers in the *Official Guide of the Railways*. It was still possible to ride a Pullman system similar to that which existed in the company's heyday of the 1920s, even if the number of Pullman lines was shrinking. All told, over 750 trains still handled Pullman cars daily in the early 1950s.

Sleeping-car passengers aboard Burlington Northern's eastbound *North Coast Limited* are enjoying the dome area of their Vista-Dome sleeper-buffet-lounge car. Perched on a Mississippi River bluff at East Dubuque, Illinois, the photographer has his own unique viewpoint of one of these interesting cars. The date is July 26, 1970, and within a year, the *North Coast Limited* will be history; Amtrak would acquire all 11 *NCL* dome sleepers. ROBERT P. SCHMIDT

ALL-PULLMAN TRAINS

At the top of the pecking order was the all-Pullman train. The term "All Pullman" lent an air of superiority to a railroad's train, denoting a run on which only first-class service was offered, often accompanied by a number of amenities such as top-flight cuisine and sometimes an on-board barber shop, maid-manicurist, valet, or train secretary. In the early 1950s, numerous all-Pullman trains still operated. In the West, the Santa Fe featured not one but two of them on its Chicago–Los Angeles route, the *Chief* and the *Super Chief*. The latter was the preferred travel choice of Hollywood celebrities into the early 1960s; they expected to be heavily pampered en route, and they were. Pullman and railroad conductors routinely made hotel and limousine arrangements for stars riding the train and once held the crack *Super Chief* for several minutes mid-route while actor Vincent Price dealt with the news of his father's death via a pay phone. Sensitive to the private needs of the stars, Santa Fe reserved the private dining room—the Turquoise Room—on the *Super Chief* for an entire trip so a feuding Richard Burton and Elizabeth Taylor wouldn't have to be seen in public. A Pullman conductor confessed that he used to share his dessert with Paul Newman when Newman's studio harassed him about his diet!

Between San Francisco/Oakland and Los Angeles, Southern Pacific operated the sophisticated all-Pullman overnight *Lark* whose feature car was a triple-unit diner-

BELOW: One of only 15 dome-sleepers built, Northern Pacific No. 311 was delivered by the Budd Company in 1954 and placed in service on the *North Coast Limited*. By 1957, 11 of the cars were in service on this train. Each car had 4 duplex roomettes and 4 double bedrooms on the main level, 4 duplex single rooms under the dome, and 24 seats in the dome. Beginning in the winter of 1959–60, when traffic on the *NCL* was low, several of the cars were released for assignment to the Illinois Central's *City of Miami* and painted in that road's distinctive orange and rust brown color scheme. They were returned to NP's two-tone green for summer operation on the *NCL*. Periodically, thereafter, several of the cars would appear during the winter on the *City of Miami* or *Panama Limited* in IC livery; they were also used on Pennsylvania Railroad's Chicago–Florida *South Wind*. Six of the cars were converted into sleeper-dome-lounges in 1967 by installing a cocktail lounge in the dome and removing two of the duplex single bedrooms in favor of a buffet. *HARRY STEGMAIER COLLECTION*

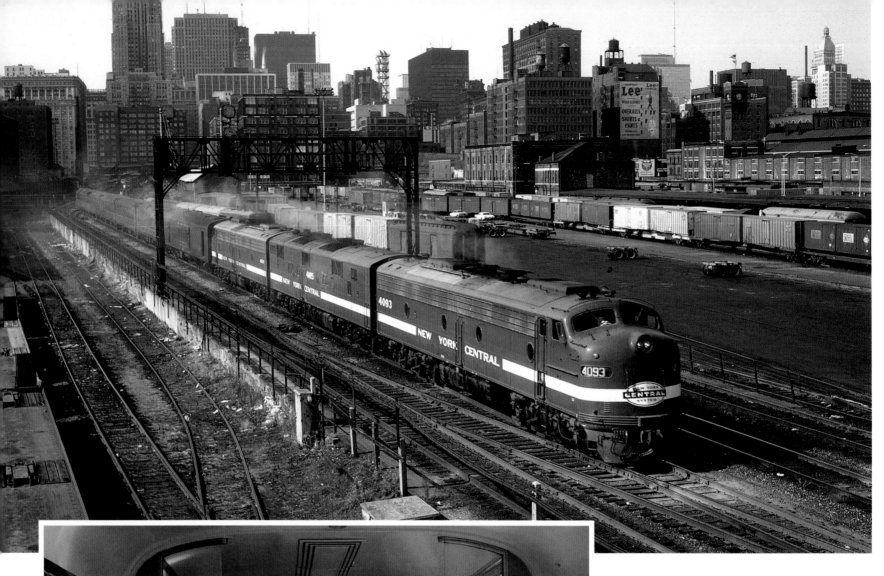

ABOVE: The chief competitor of Pennsylvania Railroad's *Broadway Limited* between Chicago and New York was New York Central's *20th Century Limited*, shown departing Chicago in the mid-1960s. Although once the most esteemed of all-Pullman trains, the *Century* lost the that title early on, in 1958, when it was combined with the *Commodore Vanderbilt*, a coach-and-Pullman train. Further, NYC ended its contract with Pullman that same year. Eventually, the *Commodore* name was dropped, but the coaches remained. *GEORGE SPEIR*

LEFT: The *Century*'s Pullman observation cars featured large picture windows and were a favorite of the train's business clientele. This interior view illustrates the sophisticated, if somewhat severe, look of the solarium end of a remodeled *Century* sleeper-observation car. *ALAN BRADLEY*

lounge—another hangout for Hollywood stars. A companion train was SP's all-Pullman *Cascade* between Oakland and Portland, Oregon.

In the brutally competitive New York–Chicago market, New York Central's *20th Century Limited*—dubbed the most famous train in the world (complete with a barber shop and train secretary who kept a "sailing list" of passengers, much like the great ocean liners) was backstopped by another NYC all-Pullman run, the *Commodore Vanderbilt*. Their direct competitors, the Pennsylvania Railroad's *Broadway Limited* and *General*, was also all-Pullman. A few dozen miles from the *Broadway's* nightly route, B&O operated the exquisite all-Pullman *Capitol Limited* on a Washington–Chicago alignment. All of these trains primarily catered to business clientele.

Like the *Capitol Limited*, Illinois Central's swank all-Pullman *Panama Limited* between Chicago and New Orleans was renowned for its cuisine. It shared a platform (after 1954) at the Crescent City with Southern/L&N's New Orleans–New York City *Crescent* which operated as an all-Pullman run east of Atlanta, adding coaches there for the daylight run to and from New Orleans. Despite the steady, early decline in parlor-car patronage, a Pullman-operated all-parlor-car train survived until June 1949 when New Haven finally added coaches to its New York–Boston *Merchant's Limited*, whose pedigree dated from 1903. It was rumored, tongue in cheek, that New Haven could have covered the *Merchant's* operating expenses simply from the on-board bar receipts garnered from its thirsty business clientele, many of whom were regular commuters on the train.

SEASONAL TRAINS

Seasonal all-Pullman trains still played a significant role in American transportation in the early 1950s and no place saw more seasonal trains than Florida, which drew a tide of migration from the North each winter. Atlantic Coast Line offered the *Florida Special* (a favorite since 1888) and the mostly heavyweight *Miamian* (which occasionally did carry coaches). Meanwhile, the Seaboard Air Line Railroad ran one of the finest, heavyweight, all-Pullman trains each winter, the seductively named *Orange Blossom Special*. Introduced in 1925, this great train ran its last mile in 1953, a victim of the marketing punch of the *Florida Special's* new streamlined equipment.

To Ellsworth, Maine, with a ferry connection to cool, seaside Bar Harbor went the summer-season-only *Bar Harbor Express* comprised largely of heavyweight Pullmans from sweltering East Coast cities like New York, Philadelphia, and Washington. The *Bar Harbor* and the *Orange Blossom* were examples of trains that benefited

Continued on page 132

Once decorated primarily in somber Pullman green, heavyweight cars increasingly received new colors in the postwar period. Perhaps the rarest heavyweight paint scheme of all time was the maroon and gray applied to cars operating in Seaboard's *Orange Blossom Special* for the 1951–52 winter season. The train was discontinued in 1953, but the exotic cars repainted for it could still be found operating in other Pullman assignments as far away as Canada. *GEHRITT BRUINS, VIA ART RIORDAN, JOE WELSH COLLECTION*

127

One of Pullman's highest revenue generators, the Santa Fe Railroad still operated two all-Pullman trains in the postwar era, both from Chicago to Los Angeles. One of those trains, the *Chief*, inaugurated in 1926, is shown during its scheduled station stop at San Bernardino, California, in a classic night shot taken by photographer Robert Hale in the early 1950s. Westbound, the *Chief* had a one-night-out schedule between Chicago and Los Angeles. The *Chief* had coaches added to it's consist in 1954. Its all-Pullman running mate, the *Super Chief*, was combined with the all-coach *El Capitan* during the off-travel season beginning in 1958. *ROBERT O. HALE, COLLECTION OF MAC MC CARTER VIA JOE WELSH*

ABOVE: Baltimore & Ohio sleeper-buffet-observation car *Genesee River* is pictured on the Baltimore–Washington–St. Louis *National* in 1965. Three of these beautiful cars, all in the *River* series—*Genesee River, Maumee River* and *Wabash River*—were built by Pullman-Standard in 1939 for New York Central's New York–Cleveland–St. Louis *Southwestern Limited.* The cars each contained 2 double bedrooms, 1 compartment and 1 drawing room, plus a buffet lounge in the observation end. They were reassigned in 1942 to the Central's *20th Century Limited,* replacing for the duration of World War II cars of somewhat lower sleeping capacity. After the war, this equipment saw a variety of assignments, including extra sections of the *Century* and Pullman pool service. In 1956 the three cars were sold to the B&O, which painted them in its regal blue-and-gray scheme. The railroad even went so far as to apply its name in raised metal script on the cars' flanks at their observation end before assigning them to its *National Limited. ALAN BRADLEY*

The *National Limited* was initially a Jersey City–Washington–St. Louis train, but was cut back to Baltimore in 1958. As patronage dwindled, the *National*'s consist correspondingly shrunk, although the *River* observation cars remained until June 1965, except for periods between 1962 and 1964 when they were replaced by other sleeper-lounge cars. As a result of B&O's 1963 affiliation with the Chesapeake & Ohio, the *National*'s through-car operation to St. Louis was integrated with the C&O's *George Washington* between Washington and Cincinnati in September 1965 and the *George Washington* name adopted for the resulting Washington–St. Louis service. At the same time, the *National* was reconfigured as an overnight train between Baltimore–Washington–Cincinnati serving local communities along its traditional B&O route. Trailing its normal consist of a combined coach and baggage car and a coach was one of the *River* cars offering Pullman-operated sleeping accommodations and restaurant car service. Since only two *River* cars were required for this operation, the third—*Genesee River*—was retired in early 1966 and transferred to the B&O Railroad Museum in Baltimore, where, unfortunately, it was destroyed several years later by vandals. The sleeper-restaurant car service on the *National* was terminated in August 1967. Although the *Wabash River* was destroyed in a derailment, *Maumee River* was sold to a private party and eventually returned to service as an officers' car for a group of shortline railroads. *ALAN BRADLEY*

Continued from page 127

ABOVE: Pullman has substituted a Chesapeake & Ohio 10-6 sleeper for the usual Erie Railroad 10-6 on the *Erie-Lackawanna Limited*, pausing during its Hoboken-to-Chicago journey at Endicott, New York, in November 1960. The C&O car, the *City of Charlottesville*, was part of a huge order—56 cars—of 10-6s that Pullman-Standard built for C&O in 1950. *CAL'S CLASSICS*

RIGHT: With the break up of Pullman, the railroads owned sleeping cars and leased them back to Pullman for staffing and operation. Although hundreds of heavyweight Pullmans received new railroad colors as a result, finding one in C&O blue, gray, and yellow was a great rarity. Most C&O heavyweights had been sold south of the border by 1950 as the railroad almost completely re-equipped its passenger fleet. *New River Gorge* is at Hamlet, North Carolina, in November 1958. *BOB'S PHOTO, WILLIAM F. HOWES JR. COLLECTION*

from Pullman's maintenance of a national pool of sleeping cars. In the spring, cars idled when the *Orange Blossom* stopped running were put to work on the *Bar Harbor Express*.

Midwesterners had their own summer-season train in the Pennsy's *Northern Arrow* which ferried a generous string of Pullmans from Chicago, St. Louis, and Cincinnati each summer to Michigan's resort area, Mackinaw City.

EVERYDAY PULLMAN SERVICE

Hundreds of other trains with a mixture of both coaches and Pullmans served a wide array of markets. And as beautiful as the all-Pullman trains and the new streamliners were, it was the ordinary, work-a-day runs

that brought Pullman into the lives of the average American. The typical overnight train in America in the early 1950s ran on medium-distance corridors connecting major city pairs like Chicago–St. Louis, Los Angeles–Oakland/San Francisco, Chicago–Minneapolis, Boston–Washington, and New York–Pittsburgh. These trains featured fast, reliable schedules that offered Pullman service to endpoint cities as well as those in between, and heavyweight sleeping cars were still quite common. A respectable number of set-out Pullman lines also survived. Set-out sleepers served larger cities using trains that passed through at inconvenient hours. For example, in 1950 a passenger could board a 14-section set-out sleeper standing at the Chicago, Rock Island & Pacific depot at Rock Island, Ill., at 9:30 p.m. and retire for the night in a cozy bed that had been made down by the porter. At 3:10 a.m., the *La Salle Street Limited* rolled in from Omaha, picked up the car, and continued on to Chicago for a 7:35 a.m. arrival at La Salle Street Station where our passenger detrained, rested from a full night's sleep. The reverse procedure happened as the 14-section car left Chicago at 1 a.m. on nameless train 9, which set out the car at Rock Island at 6:25 a.m. before continuing on to Des Moines, Iowa, No. 9's terminal. Passengers could remain aboard the Rock Island setout sleeper until 8 a.m.

It wasn't just the schedules that were convenient in the early 1950s. Pullman still reached into remote corners of America, too. Dedicated sleeper lines served places like Emporium, Pennsylvania; Lake Charles, Louisiana; Woodsville, Vermont; West Yellowstone, Montana; or Walla Walla, Washington. They also went out of country to Halifax, Nova Scotia; Mexico City, Mexico; Winnipeg, Manitoba; and other far-flung destinations.

The quality of service you received on board a Pullman didn't differ perceptibly from that in an all-Pullman train to that single car set out in Rock Island, Ill. No matter the hour or the weather, your smiling Pullman porter would greet you at the door and show you to your accommodation where crisp sheets and a perfectly made bed awaited.

ECONOMIC DECLINE

This comfortable, convenient way of life was disappearing rapidly due to subsidized competition as well as the harsh economics of the business. The massive fixed costs that were indigenous to the railroad passenger business, coupled with increasing inflation that hampered railroads' ability to raise fares and

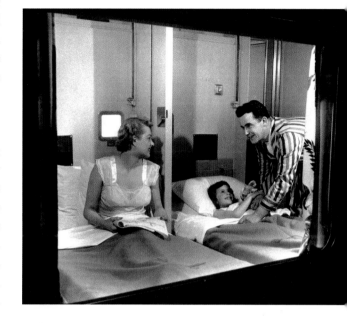

As the demand for most sleeping-car accommodations declined, the popularity of the double bedroom remained relatively strong. Although the rooms came in various floor plans, one of the last designs is depicted in these photographs of sleepers delivered to the C&O in 1950. The "day" configuration (FAR LEFT) featured two movable chairs and provisions for a portable table. While toilet facilities were in an enclosed annex, a mirrored sink alcove was accessible from within the room. Converted for night use (LEFT), upper and lower berths ran crosswise to the car. The two chairs could be folded away under the lower berth. By removing the partition between two of the rooms, a large "suite" (ABOVE) was formed that could easily accommodate a family of four.
WILLIAM F. HOWES JR. COLLECTION

ABOVE: One of the last cars in the country built with nothing but section accommodations, *Alpine Camp* was in a series of 14 cars outshopped in 1954 by American Car & Foundry for assignment to Union Pacific's *Challenger* and the *City of Portland*. By 1959, when this shot was taken, it was assigned to the B&O. *BOB'S PHOTO, WILLIAM F. HOWES JR. COLLECTION*

The Wabash was one of Pullman's last customers for parlor-car service, and it operated Pullman's most exotic parlor car—dome parlor No. 1602, with the "Blue Bird Room" lounge—on its exquisite daytime train, the *Blue Bird*, between Chicago and St. Louis. The car was an add-on to the original *Blue Bird* streamliner's all-Budd, fluted stainless-steel rolling stock. Parlor service was in high demand on the new train, enough to prompt Wabash to approach Budd for an additional parlor car. But because Budd indicated it could not quickly fulfill this special order, Wabash turned to Pullman-Standard. *PULLMAN-STANDARD, BOMBARDIER CORPORATION, JOE WELSH COLLECTION*

recover expenses, was a deadly combination. In 1955, even after significant layoffs, Pullman still employed 18,000 people and maintained a fleet of over 4,000 cars, nearly 3,000 of which were in daily service. There was little the company could do to address the cost issue. Each in-service car required a porter to operate it, and a Pullman conductor was also assigned to trains on which more than two Pullmans were carried. But the largest costs came from the behind-the-scenes efforts to maintain and manage the fleet. This labor-intensive and heavily regulated business suffered from ever-increasing costs. Between 1942 and 1954, for example, the average hourly pay rate of employees in the American railroad passenger business rose 125 percent but revenue per passenger mile increased only 39 percent.

Pullman's owner railroads were suffering too. In 1951, Pullman's two biggest clients, the New York Central and the Pennsylvania Railroad, lost $54 million and $71 million, respectively, on passenger service. Even as the railroads eliminated unprofitable trains or whole routes, Pullman sometimes found that the carriers still were contributing to its deficit by insisting on maintaining

unprofitable services, either due to the politics of being unable to eliminate a particular service or the fact that the railroad prescribed car types (such as lounges) that had limited revenue space for sale.

Nonetheless, Pullman realized that its deficits were principally due to one overriding fact: it was losing customers. Pullman ridership had been declining steadily since 1946 with the exception of the Korean War years of 1951 and 1952. In 1946, Pullman had operated 5,500 cars; by 1956 the number had been cut by more than half to just over 2,600 cars. Overall ridership had dropped by over 4 million from 1950 to 1955. More importantly, with one exception (1948), Pullman's average annual operating expenses would exceed its operating revenues as a company every year from 1946 to 1968.

In a poignant 1956 address, Pullman Vice President-Operating George Bohannon summed it up, saying, "All it would take to put us back on the profit side as far as our own accounting is concerned would be one or two more passengers per average car (per) day."

Pullman wouldn't get the chance. Seeking to attract more customers, the company had conducted a detailed

Much of the equipment on Norfolk & Western's *St. Louis Limited,* shown backing into St. Louis Union Station on August 4, 1966, is still lettered for the Wabash Railroad, former operator of this overnight Detroit–St. Louis train. On the rear is Pullman *Western Sunset,* a 12-roomette 4-double-bedroom sleeper, one of 10 12-4s built by ACF in 1950 for the Wabash. Four of the cars, all with "Western" prefixes, initially were assigned to the Union Pacific-Wabash *City of St. Louis* running between St. Louis and Los Angeles. The remaining six cars carried "Blue" names—e.g., *Blue Skies, Blue Boy, Blue Gazelle*—and were intended for general service on the Wabash's own night trains. The *Western* cars were delivered in UP yellow and gray, but by the time of this photo, *Western Sunset* had been pulled from *City* train service, repainted solid dark blue, and reassigned. *MIKE SCHAFER*

marketing study in 1953. It found that, even prior to the advent of the Interstate, 70 percent of total intercity travel occurred by auto; bus accounted for 18.1 percent of the trips; rail coach 9.8 percent; the airlines, 1.4 percent; and Pullman just 0.7 percent. The devil was in the details. Well before the appearance of reliable, fast jet travel in 1958, 60 percent of business people, Pullman's prime customers, already preferred the speed of a prop airliner to the reliability and comfort of a Pullman for business trips. Just 24 percent rode in Pullmans and 12 percent preferred the auto.

Attempting to lure frugal passengers to a service many perceived was too expensive, the railroads and Pullman introduced new budget-room-type sleeping cars. With smaller, more Spartan single- and two-person rooms than a standard roomette or bedroom, the cars—built by Budd and called "Slumbercoaches" when operated by Pullman—first appeared on Burlington's *Denver Zephyr*, which was re-equipped in 1956—the last traditional overnight streamliner re-equipped prior to the demise of Pullman 13 years hence. Newly built budget-room cars also appeared on the B&O, Missouri Pacific, Northern Pacific, and New York Central. Some other roads (UP and ACL) followed suit using existing roomette cars and lowering the asking price for the rooms. The budget-room cars were popular on most of the lines but didn't reverse the decline in Pullman traffic.

Continued on page 142

ABOVE: Florida travel generated significant Pullman business until the last days of the company. The last winter seasonal Florida train to operate was the *Florida Special* which ran from 1888 to 1972. Still comprised largely of sleeping cars and still featuring a recreation car with games and other diversions for passengers, the *Special* is shown here near Coleman, Florida, in March 1968 sporting an observation car from the *Crescent* on the rear. Winter seasonal trains often ran with an assortment of cars borrowed from other roads whose traffic declined in the off season. Note the Pennsylvania and Union Pacific cars two and three cars ahead of the observation car. DAVID W. SALTER COLLECTION OF JOE WELSH

LEFT: This view of Great Northern's eastbound *Empire Builder* on Marias Pass in Montana in 1963 was shot from one of the train's Pullman cars. Pullman traffic on some Western trains remained strong into the 1960s. LEE PHOTO, COLLECTION OF ALAN BRADLEY

RIGHT: Mexico was the eventual destination of hundreds of retired heavyweight (and ligthweight) Pullman cars in the 1960s, and a visit to Mexico in the 1950s and 1960s—even the 1970s—was like riding a time machine. Here a former American heavyweight Pullman, apparently in set-out service, is about to be shunted into the consist of a Nacionales de Mexico train in 1963—by a steam locomotive, no less. Note the former New York Central observation car—a standout in a country where Pullman green sleeping cars and steam locomotion still ruled. Pullman service in Mexico lasted until 1970, although sleeping-car service lasted well beyond that, being operated by the railroads themselves, as was the case in the U.S. Now, Mexico has been largely shorn of rail passenger service. *JOHN DZIOBKO*

BELOW: With steam power at the head of the train, a mostly heavyweight coach section (save for a single lightweight coach), and a single heavyweight Pullman-operated sleeper at the rear, this scene has all the earmarks of having been taken in the U.S. in the 1940s. Of course, the "Nacionales de Mexico" on the letterboard tells us that this is Mexico and not the U.S. The date is 1963 and heavyweight passenger cars (and steam) still ruled south of the U.S. border. In the late 1970s and early 1980s, some Mexican railways were known to charter these heavyweight Pullman relics to Americans who still yearned for a night aboard a classic steel sleeping car. *JOHN DZIOBKO*

Complete List of Sleeping Cars

OPERATING VIA

UNION PACIFIC RAILROAD

No. 59

REVISED TO JUNE 1, 1962

WESTBOUND STANDARD SLEEPING CARS

FROM	Car No.	Pullman Line No.	CAPACITY	ROUTE AND TRAIN NUMBER		Leave Daily	Arrive Daily	REMARKS	Train No.	Car No.
Chicago to										
Los Angeles	1036	4364	11 Dbl. Bdrm.					Daily		1046
Los Angeles	1033	4363	10 Roomettes, 6 Dbl. Bdrm.	CMStP&P 103, UP 103	Domeliner "City of Los Angeles"	6:00PM Sun.	10:15AM Tue.		104	1043
Los Angeles	1037	4379	5 Dbl. Bdrm., 2 Compt., 2 DR.							1047
Los Angeles	*1034*	*4380*	*10 Roomettes, 6 Dbl. Bdrm.*					*(Seasonal)*		*1044*
Los Angeles	*1032*	*4381*	*2 DR., 4 Compt., 4 Dbl. Bdrm.*					*(Seasonal)*		*1042*
San Francisco	1016	4361	2 DR., 4 Compt., 4 Dbl. Bdrm.							1026
San Francisco	*1015*	*4361*	*2 DR., 4 Compt., 4 Dbl. Bdrm.*	CMStP&P 101, UP 101, SP 101	Domeliner "City of San Francisco"	6:00PM Sun.	11:20AM Tue.	*(Seasonal)*	102	1025
San Francisco	1013	4360	10 Rmtte, 6 Dbl. Bdrm.					Daily		1023
San Francisco	1012	4362	10 Roomettes, 6 Dbl. Bdrm.							1022
Portland	1051	4370	10 Roomettes, 6 Dbl. Bdrm.	CMStP&P 105, UP 105	Domeliner "City of Portland"	3:00PM Sun.	9:00AM Tue.	Daily	106	1061
Portland	1053	4366	11 Dbl. Bdrm.							1063
Portland	1050	4367	10 Rmtte, 6 Dbl. Bdrm.							1060
Omaha to										
Los Angeles	1039	4349	10 Roomettes, 6 Dbl. Bdrm.	UP 103	Domeliner "City of Los Angeles"	2:45AM Mon.	10:15AM Tue.	(Occupancy 9:30PM)	104	1049
Los Angeles	75	658	6 Sec., 6 Rmtte., 4 Dbl. Bdrm.	UP 1-5		10:45AM Mon.	5:00AM Wed.	(Occupancy 7:00AM)	6-8	68
St. Louis to										
Los Angeles	94	685	6 Rmtte., 4 Dbl. Bdrm., 6 Sec.	Wab. 209, UP 9	Domeliner "City of St. Louis"	4:05PM Sun.	1:00PM Tue.	Daily	10-210	104
San Francisco	92	655	6 Sec., 6 Rmtte., 4 Dbl. Bdrm.	Wab. 209, UP 9, SP 27			12:40PM Tue.		28-10-210	288
Kansas City to										
Los Angeles	91	676	10 Roomettes, 6 Dbl. Bdrm.	UP 9—Domeliner "City of St. Louis"		9:20PM Sun.	1:00PM Tue.	Daily	10	101
Denver	93	639	6 Sec., 6 Rmtte., 4 Dbl. Bdrm.			7:30AM	7:50AM Mon.		10	103
Portland	170	647	6 Sec., 6 Rmtte., 4 Dbl. Bdrm.	UP 17—Portland Rose		7:30AM Sun.	5:30AM Tue.	(Occupancy 7:30AM)	18	180

ABOVE: Budd built 50 *Pacific*-series sleepers for Union Pacific in 1950. They were assigned systemwide. Although constructed of stainless steel, UP chose to paint them in Armour yellow and gray. For the majority of their service life, the sturdy cars would be owned by Amtrak and continue in revenue service to the new millennium. HARRY STEGMAIER COLLECTION

LEFT: An internal UP document from 1962 lists specific sleeping cars, configuration, Pullman line assignments, endpoints, and schedules of Pullmans serving on UP far-flung passenger network. MIKE SCHAFER COLLECTION

BELOW: UP partnered with Southern Pacific in providing service to the San Francisco Bay area. This blunt-end SP 10-6 sleeper was built as the tail car for the *City of San Francisco* and wore UP's Armour yellow and gray required for cars regularly used in City train service. HARRY STEGMAIER COLLECTION

BELOW: Chicago & North Western was a partner with UP in Chicago–West Coast train service until October 1955 when UP shifted operation of the Chicago–Omaha portion of its transcontinental trains to The Milwaukee Road. Here, *Villa Road*, a 1930 rebuild with 10 sections and 3 double bedrooms, is pictured painted in Armour yellow and gray for UP assignment. The car was purchased from Pullman in 1948 by C&NW. *JOHN S. INGLES*

Continued from page 137

Pullman's business continued to unravel. In 1956 the Pennsylvania, New Haven, and the Wabash—the last railroads using Pullman to operate their parlor cars—took over the service themselves. In 1958 NYC, at one time Pullman's largest customer, took over all its local sleeping-car lines itself. The only Pullman lines Central continued to operate were interline services with the C&O.

The network of Pullman car lines that had once made the passenger trains convenient now began disappearing rapidly from small and medium-sized American towns. The cost of maintaining a sleeping-car line with a porter often outstripped the revenue to be earned. Where it was possible to eliminate the cars, the railroads and Pullman did so. As the 1960s dawned, the Pullman sleeping-car system essentially retrenched to providing only point-to-point service to larger cities aboard a dwindling number of overnight trains. The set-out sleeper had almost vanished.

One example of this decline could be found on the Delaware, Lackawanna & Western Railroad. Not one of Pullman's larger customers, for years the Lackawanna had nevertheless provided a network of reliable night trains and sleeping cars to many communities along its lines in New Jersey, Pennsylvania, and New York. Like its richer brethren, the Lackawanna had even equipped with streamlined sleeping cars in the late 1940s. Almost immediately thereafter the road began to pare down its money-losing services. On July 21, 1951, Hoboken, New Jersey–Scranton, Pennsylvania, sleeping-car service was discontinued; on August 1, 1956, Hoboken–Detroit, Michigan, Pullman service via the New York Central at Buffalo was terminated. On August 10, 1957, Hoboken–Syracuse, New York, and Philadelphia–Syracuse sleeper service (via the Reading Railroad between Philadelphia and Scranton) ended. All of these car lines had been protected by older, heavyweight cars, but even as late as 1958, Lackawanna still provided eight Pullman car lines using lightweight cars, including at least three set-out sleeper lines to State of New York destinations like Elmira, Binghamton, and Buffalo. The opening of the New York State Thruway and the growth of Mohawk Airlines began to take its toll shortly thereafter. Cash starved, the Lackawanna merged with the Erie in 1960; by the end of 1963, all of its remaining sleeping-car lines had vanished from the timecard. It was like that all over America.

Illinois Central *Sugarland* is a 6-section 6-roomette 4-double-bedroom car, one of 12 such sleepers with Southern-themed names (e.g., *Banana Road, Land O' Strawberries, Magnolia State*) built by Pullman-Standard in 1942 for the newly streamlined *Panama Limited* between Chicago/St. Louis and New Orleans. After World War II, these cars were bumped to other services by new 10-6s as the *Panama* became an all-room train. In this bucolic scene along the Cedar River in Waterloo, Iowa, on June 2, 1956, the *Sugarland* is in set-out sleeper service for IC's Chicago–Sioux City, Iowa, *Hawkeye.* Westbound, the car was dropped at dawn in Waterloo, and its occupants could remain in their beds until 8 a.m. Eastbound, the car was ready for occupancy at 9:30 p.m., with the Chicago-bound *Hawkeye* picking it up just before midnight. This Waterloo set-out service was gone by the end of the 1950s, but 6-6-4s would continue to protect the Chicago–Sioux City Pullman line until the mid-1960s, after which a 10-6 was usually assigned until Pullman service on IC's Western Lines ended altogether in 1968.
JOHN HUMISTON, MIKE SCHAFER COLLECTION

The letters began pouring into the railroads about service that had been discontinued or the fact that what was once a convenient trip with a 10 p.m. departure now required driving a hundred miles to a larger station and then boarding a Pullman in the middle of the night. The railroads were hemorrhaging cash and, frankly, had made up their mind that the service had to go.

By now, Pullman's largest customer was the huge

Pennsylvania Railroad. While the Lackawanna exemplified the loss of service to small-town America, Pennsy's inexorable abandonment of Pullman underscored the loss of sleeping-car service to two major regions of the country, the Northeast and the Midwest. In 1960, PRR handled 234 regularly assigned Pullman sleeping cars and 86 spares (belonging to PRR and its partner roads) covering 156 different Pullman lines. The lines stretched from the East Coast as far west as St. Louis on the PRR or via other roads as far south as Florida, as far north as Montreal and as far west as Texas. They were, by now, almost exclusively covered by lightweight cars, and the vast majority of the lines went to major destinations—the railroad having aggressively eliminated Pullman service to the many small towns it once served on its vast network of track east of Chicago and St. Louis.

According to 1962 accounting records, Pullman spent $157 per day to operate each car and earned about $136. On that basis, it was losing nearly $315,000 a year on the operations (in 1962 dollars). By the end of 1967, Pennsy would operate just 19 local sleeping-car lines and 39 interline lines (of which 11 were seasonal) handed off to connecting roads that had healthier ridership, such as the Seaboard Coast Line to Florida. At the time, Western roads and the Florida railroads continued to carry a substantial number of sleeping-car patrons. And there were still anomalies such as the SCL's popular *Silver Meteor*, handling eight Pullman sleeping cars a night to Florida or the Union Pacific's little remarked *Butte Special* providing sleeping-car and even Pullman meal service (one of the

last in the country) to far flung outposts in Montana. But PRR's decline in service more closely mirrored that of many other lines across the country.

Facing large deficits and attempting to reduce expenses for its upcoming merger with New York Central, Pennsy asked Pullman to provide a "partial form of service" on its local lines and later on the New Haven Railroad as well. Specifically, Pullman would continue to furnish, clean, repair, and stock the cars with supplies, and the railroad would staff them and handle the ticketing. On August 1, 1967, the new arrangement became effective.

RIGHT: In a mock-up scene staged at the Pullman plant near Chicago in 1950, Pullman trainmen assist "passengers" alighting from Nickel Plate sleepers. *THE PULLMAN COMPANY, WILLIAM F. HOWES JR. COLLECTION*

BELOW: A Nickel Plate steam switcher is in the middle of reshuffling the consist of NKP's Chicago–Buffalo *City of Cleveland* streamliner at Cleveland in 1956. Here, the Chicago–Cleveland 10-roomette 6-double-bedroom sleeper (next to locomotive) will be dropped from the train as will the 5-double-bedroom buffet-lounge next to it; another 10-6 (not in view) will continue through to Hoboken, New Jersey, via the Lackawanna Railroad east of Buffalo. NKP bought 13 10-6 sleepers and 2 sleeper-lounges in 1950 for Chicago–Cleveland–Hoboken service. *JOHN DZIOBKO*

Due to rising costs, numerous other railroads, in 1968, asked Pullman to operate a "partial form of service." Soon, a majority of the railroads came to prefer this arrangement. Pullman then advised all its railroads that it had become impractical and uneconomical to continue providing attendant service. As a result, most of the remaining railroads switched over to the partial-service method, although a few, such as the Missouri Pacific, chose to simply terminate all sleeping-car service on their lines. On January 1, 1969, Pullman ceased providing porter service on board all the remaining sleeping cars operating in the U.S. Regularly scheduled Pullman service had ended in Canada in 1966. On February 1, 1969, all of Pullman's remaining railroads served notice that they wished to cancel their uniform service contracts for the partial form of service. Effective August 1, 1969, Pullman ceased operation in the United States. It was the end of an era for an exceptionally comfortable, service-oriented transportation option.

9 ways to travel in comfort

by PULLMAN

YOU'RE SAFE AND SURE
WHEN YOU TRAVEL BY
Pullman
. . . COSTS LESS THAN YOU THINK!

TOP: In a last-ditch effort to attract riders, Pullman and the railroads introduced "Slumbercoaches" in the 1950s. They offered smaller, low-cost rooms at a modest charge over coach fares. B&O's *Slumberland*, shown with a stewardess-nurse at Baltimore's Camden Station in 1958, is one of two Budd Slumbercoaches (the other was *Dreamland*) acquired by B&O that year and leased to Pullman, which initially operated them on the *Columbian* and later the *Capitol Limted*. BALTIMORE & OHIO, WILLIAM F. HOWES JR. COLLECTION

ABOVE: Pullman's new (and final) logo. MIKE SCHAFER COLLECTION

LEFT: Pullman's last promotional folders, issued in the 1960s, were simple one-fold affairs that, in essence, preached to the choir. Ridership never fully recovered after World War II. MIKE SCHAFER COLLECTION

147

6

On December 31, 1968, the Pullman Company closed its doors to U.S. passengers. The experience of riding a Pullman-operated car was no longer available in the United States. But despite Pullman's demise, sleeping-car service itself continued to be offered by a number of railroads that simply assumed that job the day Pullman ceased to operate sleeping-car service. Among the largest private railroad operators of sleeping cars were the Seaboard Coast Line, linking Florida with the Northeast, and the Union Pacific, which operated trains from Chicago to the West Coast via a connection with the Milwaukee Road between Chicago and Omaha. Both railroads maintained large fleets of sleepers which they staffed themselves after the demise of Pullman and before the arrival of Amtrak in 1971. Other railroads such as the Missouri Pacific that had far fewer first-class customers and less reason to assume the full expense of operating sleepers abandoned the operation of all sleeping cars concurrent with Pullman's closing.

On May 1, 1971, Amtrak, a quasi-public company whose formation was authorized and partially funded by the federal (and later also state) governments, took over the responsibility of operating a skeletal system of intercity passenger trains. The last holdout to operate its own sleeping-car service in the U.S. was the Southern Railway, which didn't join Amtrak until 1979. From 1971 to 1979, Southern

Former Missouri Pacific car 655, the *Eagle Forest*, headed south of the border when MP opted out of sleeping-car operation in the late 1960s. The car is shown as Sonora Baja California 5017, the *Nabor Flores*, at Mexicali, Mexico, in March 1974. The 14-roomette, 4-double-bedroom car was one of six 14-4s built by Pullman-Standard in 1948 for MP subsidiary International Great Northern for service on the *Texas Eagle* and *Louisiana Eagle*. The three wide ribs on the car sides were a MP hallmark.

PAUL C. HUNNELL

operated the *Southern Crescent* between Washington and New Orleans with a through connection to/from New York City via Amtrak; for a time, the *Southern Crescent* also handled a through, coast-to-coast (New York–Los Angles) sleeping car in conjunction with Amtrak's *Sunset Limited*. The *Crescent* remained an outstanding example of first-class railroad service, and the train's consist included sleeping cars once operated by The Pullman Company. The *Crescent* offered roomettes, double bedrooms, drawing rooms, and the largest accommodation once offered by Pullman: the master room complete with its own shower. The *Crescent's* cars were impeccably maintained and finished in interior paint schemes and upholstery reminiscent of the late Pullman era. Likewise, the excellent service aboard the trains was provided in a manner recalling a bygone era.

The new but chronically under-capitalized Amtrak was a different story. Although the national carrier acquired hundreds of sleeping cars that had once been operated by Pullman for the private railroads, there was virtually no resemblance to Pullman in either the quality of on-board service or equipment maintenance. Indeed, the new company seemed to be in a headlong rush to distance itself from the private railroads it replaced. Amtrak's original cars were—in keeping with the times, the wild and wooly 1970s—refurbished in garish, "mod" colors and patterns that assaulted the eyes and arguably had no place in the tight confines of a sleeping car. The consis-

tency of early on-board service was equally annoying. Some service provided by a number of highly trained and motivated veterans of the private railroads (and The Pullman Company) was outstanding. But generally Amtrak service in the first decade of the company was characterized by minimal attention from disinterested employees, some of whom were under-trained new hires and others who were disgruntled veterans. Maintenance was equally poor. Burdened with a fleet of older, non-standard cars, the national carrier insisted on operating them all over the country. The cars' age coupled with the fact that Amtrak expected them to be maintained by crews who had no familiarity with the mechanical systems of another railroad led to breakdowns and fleet availability problems.

Improvements for Amtrak's first-class passengers came slowly. Balky steam-heating systems eventually were replaced by standardized, reliable electrical systems on rebuilt veteran cars. Finally, in 1979, the company took delivery of the first new sleeping cars built specifically for Amtrak: the Superliner series. Loosely patterned after the double-deck cars built for Santa Fe's all-coach *El Capitan* in the mid-1950s, the new bi-level Superliners originally operated only on Western railroads where clearances were more generous. The Superliners contained intelligently designed interiors and offered a quiet, comfortable ride. On-board service was also improving although there was never the quantum leap in improvement symbolized by the arrival of new equipment.

Today, Amtrak still provides its own sleeping-car service in its fleet of Superliner (double deck) and Viewliner (single-deck) cars, all pre-Amtrak sleepers having been retired from revenue service. Although much more reliable than it once was, service levels on Amtrak sleepers does not approach the high level of quality and consistency once offered aboard a Pullman. But for the passenger seeking the privacy and convenience of regularly scheduled intercity sleeping-car travel in the U.S., today's Amtrak offers the only opportunity to savor this comfortable way to travel.

FORMER PULLMANS IN SERVICE

For those interested in luxury or historical accuracy, only a small number of restored Pullman cars, both heavyweight and lightweight, stand ready to carry passengers on custom itineraries. Perhaps the ultimate experience is the *American Orient Express*, a train comprised of many former lightweight Pullman cars and that provides luxury rail-tour service on pre-set sailing schedules. The *AOE's* cars are restored in a manner resembling European Wagons Lits sleeping cars rather than American Pullmans, but the train offers excellent service and

Early in its life, Amtrak acquired numerous sleeping cars that had been in Pullman service, such as former-Union Pacific *Pacific Scene*, a 10-6 sleeper built by the Budd Company in 1950. The car is shown getting washed at Denver Union Station while serving as one of the sleeping cars on Amtrak's westbound *San Francisco Zephyr* in March 1975. The car has received an Amtrak makeover, inside and out, that has included the removal of UP gray and yellow livery. *BOB SCHMIDT*

cuisine and a chance to see the country by rail truly in the grand manner.

If you have unlimited means or can arrange a private group tour, consider chartering your own private railroad car. For those with a passion for historical accuracy and vintage Pullman cars look no further than the *Dover Harbor*. Operated by the Washington, D.C., Chapter of the National Railway Historical Society, *Dover Harbor* was rebuilt by Pullman in 1934 to include six double bedrooms and a buffet lounge. The car is the only surviving heavyweight Pullman sleeping car still in charter service. Its interior and exterior are lovingly restored to the appearances of a heavyweight Pullman circa the 1940s. The one major concession to the ravages of time has been the replacement of the car's original riveted pedestal trucks with six-wheel cast integral-pedestal trucks from a former Canadian National lightweight sleeper.

Several attractive lightweight Pullman cars still operate in charter service. Among those that retain their basic Pullman-era external appearances are *Royal Street*, a former observation car from the *Crescent*, *Silver Solarium*, a Vista-

LEFT: Southern Railway's post-Amtrak *Southern Crescent* streamliner operating between Washington and New Orleans until 1979 (when SR joined Amtrak) was the last bastion for sleeping-car service that closely resembled that of the post-World War II Pullman era. On a humid night in the summer of 1978, the *Crescent*'s ex-Pullman sleepers shimmer in the night lights of the station at Lynchburg, Virginia. MIKE SCHAFER

BELOW: Amtrak commemorated George M. Pullman by naming one of its bilevel Superliner sleepers after him. JOHN KUEHL

BOTTOM: Faithfully restored heavyweight Pullman *Dover Harbor* riding on the rear of the *California Zephyr* arriving Chicago in 1999 provides a stark contrast to the adjacent Superliner car. JOHN H. KUEHL

Dome sleeper-observation car from the *California Zephyr*; *Vista Canyon*, a former *Super Chief* observation car; and *Pine Tree State*, a former New Haven Railroad lounge-sleeper. To some degree or another, all of the above cars have had interior remodeling done as a concession to their new roles as private charter cars.

FORMER PULLMANS IN STATIC DISPLAY

Without question, the premier heavyweight Pullman car preserved in static display in the U.S. is the *Lotos Club*, an 8-section restaurant-lounge car rebuilt by Pullman in 1936. The car was purchased and meticulously restored by historian Peter Tilp who enjoyed it for many years in private ownership. Eventually, the car was donated to the Railroad Museum of Pennsylvania at Strasburg where it can be seen today. The *Silver Crescent*, a former *California Zephyr* lightweight Vista-Dome sleeper-observation car has been restored to virtually its original appearance; it can be found at Florida's Gold Coast Railroad Museum. Among its roommates at the Gold Coast is the *Ferdinand Magellan*, a heavyweight (and heavily armored) Pullman observation car used in private service by President Franklin D. Roosevelt for much of World War II.

Although not technically a Pullman, but a car that served on the Canadian National Railways, the heavyweight sleeper displayed at the beautiful California State Railroad Museum in Sacramento comes amazingly close to recreating a journey in a heavyweight Pullman without traveling a single mile.

The car, named *St. Hyacinthe* and built in 1929 by the Canadian Car & Foundry Company of Montreal, is typical of the steel Pullman-operated sleeping cars of the heavyweight era. It contains 10 open sections, 1 drawing room, and 1 compartment.

St. Hyacinthe's exterior has been restored by the museum to its late-1940s appearance; the car's interior reflects the early 1950s. It is displayed in the nighttime configuration; some berths are made-down and a lone "passenger" is sound asleep in his compartment. But the realism extends beyond the decor. A mechanical device gently rocks the car to simulate motion, and the lights of passing towns and grade crossings flash by the windows. There is even a soundtrack which simulates the typical night sounds of a fast-moving passenger train: the rhythmic clicking of the wheels, the distant whistle of the locomotive, and the distinctive noise of passing crossing bells.

Standing in the *St. Hyacinthe* is like being transported back in time.

PULLMANS IN MINIATURE

For those seeking to enjoy the Pullman fleet on a scale smaller than 1 to 1, a fascinating variety of choices exist. Perhaps the most complete and accurate range of examples can be found in HO scale model railroading. From the expert model builders of Ajin Precision and Samhongsa of South Korea and through the diligent effort of importers such as The Coach Yard, Railway Classics, and Challenger Imports, models of amazing accuracy and flawless finish have recently become available to the connoisseur of name trains.

From the delicate pin-striping and sleek lines of lightweight cars designed by the legendary Raymond Loewy for Pennsylvania Railroad service to the solid battleship appearance of heavyweight Pullmans, a wide variety of cars and complete consists of trains are available, if briefly (all are limited-run productions), to collectors. To those with the money and the time it is possible to recreate again in miniature the days when the passenger train was king and Pullman was the way to travel.

OPPOSITE PAGE, TOP: *California Zephyr* Vista-Dome Pullman lounge-observation car *Silver Solarium* trails the rear of a whole string of private railroad cars in charter service on a trip through the American west. JOHN H. KUEHL

OPPOSITE PAGE, BOTTOM: Louisville & Nashville *Royal Street* was one of four high-windowed *Royal*-series 5-double-bedroom buffet-lounge observation cars built by Pullman-Standard in 1950 for assignment to the New York–New Orleans *Crescent*, a joint operation of L&N, Southern, Western Railway of Alabama, Atlanta & West Point, and Pennsylvania Railroad. Handsomely restored, it is shown passing through Chicago in charter service in 2002. JOHN H. KUEHL

A firm called The Coach Yard produces a range of beautiful whole train consists or individual Pullman cars in HO scale. Included are a *Night* series car (UPPER PHOTO) with 14 single bedrooms and the *George M. Pullman*, (LOWER) Pullman's first lightweight car. THE COACH YARD

Index